Rebalancing the Addictive Mind

BEATING ADDICTION WITH EXERCISE AND NUTRITION

Rochelle Ann Poerio

MA, LADC, CFT

ISBN: 1500444561
ISBN-13: 9781500444563

Dedication

To those suffering the ravages of addiction.

And those about to be.

Contents

Acknowledgments

First of all, I want to thank Neil Conway. Neil has been my editor since day one on this project, when we scratched an outline onto a couple of blank pieces of paper in the summer of 2012. Neil, thanks for helping me write what I really meant to say. And for all of your considerable time and effort.

To my mother, for helping with the editing process. I'm also eternally grateful for all of the encouragement, support and love I've received from my dad, mom, brother and sister, and their families. I'm sure it wasn't easy for them to trust, open up and believe again. Proof that time and amends can heal all wounds.

To Casey Jones for kick-starting me when I felt stuck, and bringing creativity and insight into the project.

To the countless people in the program who have touched my life, especially my sponsors.

Jill, I would never have made it without you. That's no exaggeration. Martha, thanks for helping me get over and through the countless hurdles from year two and beyond. I'm grateful every day I still have you as my sponsor. And that our calls are no longer crisis-management oriented.

There are many others who helped me at the lowest points of my early recovery, through the days of unemployment, self-doubt, fear and isolation.

I will never forget. Thank you, Patrice, Kevin and Mason.

In memoriam: Sara Hamilton, Ed Haber and Barbrady. And to John Shilling, who welcomed me to my first post-detox AA meeting, made me feel safe and comfortable, and introduced me to Jill.

Important Disclaimer

This book is intended to be an introduction to basic concepts of addiction, recovery, exercise and nutrition. This book is not medical advice. It is not intended to treat any disease or supersede any instruction, advice or direction from your medical professional. Do not start any program of exercise or nutrition without consulting with your physician first. Nutritional information contained herein is purposely limited and should not be considered absolute or definitive. Dietary guidance and sample programs are generic, purposely limited and may not be appropriate for you. Exercise activities and sample programs are generic, purposely limited, and may not be applicable to you. You and your heirs agree to hold the author and all parties named herein harmless for any failure to heed these warnings and for any negative consequences you may attribute to practicing any principle outlined in this book.

This book is for informational purposes only.

1

The Beginning of the End

Arlington, Virginia, mid-August, 2001...

The .45 caliber Beretta Cougar lies on the desk, safety on, seven in the clip, one round chambered. Water beads roll slowly down the outside of a faded, illegible 32-ounce plastic party cup.

Ugh. What the...? Zoned out again. Drunk still. What time is it? It's not unusual this summer for me to come to, see daylight and not know if its 6:00 a.m. or 6:00 p.m. I am also wondering what day it is.

I'm such a miserable loser. What is wrong with me? Why is this happening: every day, the same nightmarish routine! Why won't it stop? And why does it seem to be getting even worse? Nothing I can think of makes a difference. Nothing changes.

Is this what happens when you go crazy? But do "crazy" people know they're going crazy? This is all so damned confusing!

I look at the gun again, pick it up, run through the potential scenario... again. This can't be right. But what am I supposed to do? How could this be happening?

My cats are poking around the kitchen, looking for food. I look down. Barbrady is at my feet. His eyes seem full of tenderness and unconditional love, despite what I have become. What the f---? Big huge sobs now.

I can't take this anymore. Somehow, deep down, I know that considering blowing my brains out daily for the last two weeks is a serious problem. Trouble is, I can't figure out how to fix it. I must be descending into mental illness — maybe (hopefully?) it's a brain tumor? Wouldn't that be better than insanity? I just need to understand what has happened to my life.

Barbrady jumps on my lap. Dammit! I push him down. I'm on a roll – feeling sorry for myself – I can't be bothered to pay him any attention right now. I'm alone, ashamed, isolated. When was the last time I took a shower, or washed my hair? And why does it feel overwhelming simply to bathe or brush my teeth?

I have no friends, no job. I wake up shaking, scared and sweating in the middle of the night. The time I am unconscious is the only time I am not drinking. I have begun waking up at 3:00 a.m. in order to drink and avoid withdrawal (even though I'm in such deep denial I don't understand this is what I am doing). My actions are to alleviate anxiety that borders on panic, and the sweating and uncontrollable vomiting I endure if don't get vodka into my body immediately.

I keep imagining something will magically change, but it doesn't. In fact, it's gotten so bad in the last couple of months that I'm afraid to use any drugs for fear of some kind of bad reaction or overdose. "I'll stick with an alcohol-only policy; it's the only safe option. Besides, it's not like I have money for drugs, anyway."

Stupid cat –– bugging me again! Let me wallow in shame! Big huge uncontrollable sobs shake my body. Tears and snot run down my face. "I guess I'm just going to have to make a final decision here in the next day or two. I can't take it any longer."

Meowing, Barbrady rubs against my ankles as I sit in the worn desk chair. Louder cries; he is not going anywhere.

I set the gun back on the desk. I bend down and pull him up onto my lap. He stops mewling and starts purring, very loud. For some reason, I look above the computer screen and TV on my desk at the light filtering through the Venetian blinds onto the wall.

The light/shadow pattern is a clear contrast, geometrically pleasing, beautiful really. For a moment, I feel a connection to the world outside my misery. The brain-fog and blinding emotionality momentarily evaporate. A crystal clear thought enters my drunken, tired, and malnourished mind: "What if you're 'just' an alcoholic? What if that's all that is going on here?"

A wave of relief and calm washes over me. "What? Could it be that simple? I mean, being an alcoholic is a disgusting, shameful, pathetic thing, but that's potentially manageable, isn't it? Unlike losing one's mind, right? Hmmm. Maybe I should think about this some more."

I get up, put the gun away, walk into the kitchen and refill the filthy cup with 80 percent vodka, 20 percent club soda. "Yes, let me think about this "alcoholic" concept for a bit."

Admitting Defeat

This was the beginning of the end of my active addiction. After many hesitations, procrastinations and a seven-year relapse that brought me to this point, I was finally starting to consider that perhaps I was beaten: addiction and self-destruction had won.

In the intervening two weeks I drank, felt sorry for myself, and was frequently a demanding, impatient jack-ass, no matter what the circumstance.

"Why can't you get me in to see a primary physician today?! I have good insurance!" ("You bunch of idiot-losers! Don't you know

3

who I am? And how important *my* needs are?" was the thought process.)

Somehow, I made a doctor's appointment. Even better, I actually showed up for the appointment! Despite my best effort, I failed to convince the doc to prescribe me Klonopin® (clonazepam, a benzodiazepine) so I could go home and "treat" myself. It was at that point that I knew, in my heart of hearts, that I had had enough.

"You need to go to a hospital detox," the primary care doctor said. "OK," as my weak response. I was beaten and it was ugly. I didn't argue.

My addiction wanted to fight, but my body and mind were broken. Inertia was on the side of surrender, not battle. I was definitely afraid of the future, but I was more afraid of continuing on my current path.

Fairfax, Virginia, September 5, 2001…

I wander around the grounds of Inova Fairfax hospital, in Fairfax, Virginia, after the cabbie has dropped me off. Dragging a duffle bag, suffering withdrawal, limping because my old knee injury is acting up again, I am stopped by some random guy, who asks if I need help. "God, I must look even more pathetic than I feel!" is all I can think.

He offers to carry my duffle bag and walk me in the direction I need to go – to CATS (Comprehensive Addiction Treatment Program).

"Why would you do that?" I ask.

"Well, you look like you could use some help," he replies.

"Why would you help me?" I ask suspiciously.

"Having difficulty believing that someone might just want to help because you look like you could use a hand?" he asks.

"Yup! That sums it up," I reply testily.

"Hmmm. Well, get used to it. Come on. Follow me." He picks up my bulky duffle bag and starts marching toward the detox hospital ward. "By the way, I'm Dr. Eder; I'm going to be your physician."

With that, Day One of my recovery journey began....

Leaving the Land of the Dead

"Genetics loads the gun; environment pulls the trigger."

An 80-year-old woman named Betty in my Saturday morning women's AA meetings used to say that. I can still hear her gravelly voice. Her message continues to resonate.

It's easier than you think to get out of control, or simply to perpetuate an increasingly unhealthy lifestyle. This book is a way to understand addiction and recovery, and to find a path away from abuse of substances and/or behavioral addictions. It is not only for the "hardcore" addict or alcoholic. It can help the person who is the "weekend warrior," or the "couple pops per night" drinker/ user. The "partier" might eventually get into trouble, or go into full-blown addiction, or not. The point is that the lifestyle is certainly not healthy.

Many of the addictions-related shows on TV — "Intervention," "Dr. Drew," etc. — feature people who have become addicts and alcoholics. As we delve into their stories, there is always what may be interpreted as a built-in excuse. "I was abused as a child, my kid was killed in a car accident, my husband beats me, I am a combat veteran...that's why I use." While not to minimize the impact of trauma, it's not the whole story.

We all know people who have suffered trauma, horror and loss and who have not become addicted to anything. That fact speaks to the hereditary and genetic underpinnings of addiction.

This, plus the brain changes that develop from using, are why *addiction is a disease.* So throw away your self-pity and self-hatred. Addiction is not intrinsically a "moral failing."

Return to the Land of the Living

If you want to return to the land of the living for good, it's time to get out of the inside of your head and become open-minded and willing to listen and to act.

Without a doubt, it is hard to seek help, or treatment. It's even harder if you feel there is no hope, your situation is unique, or that you are beyond help. In order to make a decision to seek assistance, or to make a change, it's important to understand that you and your circumstances are not unique. Addictive behaviors and consequences are remarkably consistent. You are not the first person that has engaged in irresponsible, shameful, arrogant, selfish, lying, sneaky, isolation/hiding, deviant, criminal…(fill in the blanks)…behaviors and thought processes. Nor will you be the last.

Substance and process (gambling, shopping, sex, porn, internet and gaming) addictions naturally promote feelings of shame, guilt, self-loathing and self-hatred. It's easy to think of yourself as a degenerate loser when you consistently acts in ways that only promote those negative feelings. The addict always feels unique and alone in that "no one else could possibly be as (fill-in-the-blank) bad, immoral, unfaithful, degenerate, inhuman, unlovable, etc., as me." But that feeling is inaccurate. Approximately 10 percent of Americans suffer from addiction. That translates into approximately 30 million people in the U.S.! Go to any 12-step meeting. You'll find everyone in the room can pretty much tell your "story" — despite never having met you. Why? Because addiction and its consequences are their story, too!

People become addicted because they are *genetically predisposed* to addiction. Just as often, our first experiences with using happen not because of trauma or by self-medicating a condition like depression, but because drinking, using a drug, or gambling is pleasurable, or makes us feel more comfortable in our own skins.

You like having a drink. Or popping a Xanax. Or playing poker. It feels good. Unfortunately, if you have a genetic propensity for addiction, over time, you can't stop. You repeat the seemingly innocuous pleasurable or relief-bringing activity. And repeat it. And repeat it. And brain-and-body response conditioning begins. The only way to rejoin the land of the living is through abstinence and committing to change.

Addiction's Perimeter Fence

Defense mechanisms reinforce addictive thinking and behavior. Defense mechanisms in addiction are elaborate excuses and ways of behaving that protect our using and block our ability to stop. We must learn to identify these defense mechanisms and deconstruct them.

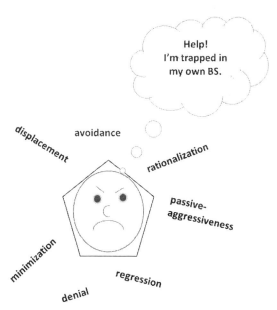

The defense mechanism nearly everyone is familiar with is *denial.* We simply deny that we have a problem. And often we complement denial with other defenses such as *rationalization,*

which is a way of justifying drug usage or behaviors. For instance, I tell you that the reason I drank heavily last night was because I was stressed at work. Or that I "deserved" a reward for completing a big project.

Rationalization fits hand-in-glove with *intellectualization*, which leverages facts and logic to support continued usage. "No, I'm not squandering my money. I spend about $100 when I go out to dinner. Instead of going out to dinner, I'm staying in. So the net financial impact of me buying a gram of coke is zero."

Another frequently used defense mechanism is *minimization*. And if I do something shameful, or dumb, just why wouldn't I attempt to under-emphasize the result or impact? "It's not a big deal that I was too hung-over to take the kids to school today. I don't know why you're upset. School was letting out early today, anyway!"

I know that one of my favorite defense mechanisms was *projection*, especially when I felt my addiction threatened by my "normal" friends. After all, who were *they* to tell me that I was using "too much" or was "over the top"? Yes, it was easy for me to attribute my negative or unhealthy qualities to another. The next time "Joe" was late for work, I was certain to mention how "Joe" was probably an incorrigible closet-drinker, who was no-doubt late because he was hung-over and sick.

Often, after being confronted, the addicted person resorts to *regression*, or reverting to immature or less civilized behaviors. Family or friends suggest that Mary has a drinking problem. Her response is yelling and screaming at them, making unfounded accusations, and running out of the house. I must say, there's nothing quite so pathetic as watching a supposedly educated, well-mannered, responsible adult behaving like a four-year-old.

Addicts and alcoholics have a way of reinforcing defense mechanisms with egocentric beliefs and by "comparing out."

My egocentric thinking tells me that what other people think, do, or say is not important and does not apply to me. My "comparing out" allows me to "prove" that my actions and behaviors are not problematic.

For instance, Melanie goes to the bar every night after work and has six drinks. When confronted by her boyfriend about her drinking, she rebels. She tells her boyfriend about their mutual friend Dave, who frequents the same bar every night and puts away 10 to 12 drinks. He frequently gets into verbal confrontations with other customers, often passes out while waiting for a taxi to pick him up, and even fell off the curb one time and dislocated his knee.

Comparing out, Melanie says, "I don't have a problem. Look at Dave! That is what a *problem* is! I don't pass out on the street! I don't get kicked out of bars!" Yet Melanie demonstrates other problematic, illegal or anti-social behavior in more passive or indirect ways. She is obviously having relationship difficulties related to her drinking. She has called in "sick" to work four times in the last six weeks because she was so hung-over. She drives home under the influence regularly. While Melanie hasn't suffered any of Dave's problems (yet!), she is minimizing, rationalizing and denying the negative consequences and potential of *her* drinking.

Melanie has cocooned herself with defense mechanisms, egocentric beliefs, and comparing out. She attempts to protect her addictive behavior by promoting a fantasy of "I don't have any problem; look at Dave. He's the degenerate!"

And after this confrontation with her boyfriend, Melanie might run upstairs and kick the dog or cat, an example of *displacement*. Melanie redirects her anger and frustration with her boyfriend's accusations onto a weaker and unwitting target. It's a way of relieving tension and anxiety without confronting the real issue.

And then there is *avoidance*. Maybe the best example of avoidance is simply using more drugs, alcohol, gambling or all of the above. "No sense in having to trouble my pretty little head with all this awfulness." Passive-aggressiveness might play into Melanie's situation. "I'll show him. I'll show him what real drinking is, if he is going to insist on being such an ass!"

These are a few of the many ways we defend our clearly unacceptable, anti-social and unhealthy behaviors. Consciously or subconsciously, we are defending against what we know must be done – that *we must stop using. We must change.*

How Did I Get Here and Which Way is Out?

A point I want to stress is that there are many paths to problem substance use or behaviors. These paths may be based in avoidance of trauma, depression and anxiety. Or they may be based in doing something "fun" that creates negative behavior patterns that harm one's lifestyle, social relationships, personal goals, or career.

But the path we all share relates to specific neurochemical changes that occur in the brain, which lead to alterations in our thinking, coping and behavior. Because severe consequences usually fail to manifest in the early stages of using, addiction is free to gain a large beachhead in the brain. The pleasurable (or relief-bringing) activity takes on ever-greater significance in the person's lifestyle and activities. The fire of obsession is being stoked. Tolerance to the drug begins to build.

Now it's not just for the occasional weekend or special function. The substance or behavioral addiction becomes a coping skill and slowly (or quickly) becomes knitted into the fabric of our lives. These changes may (and often do) become permanent. And you become assimilated by *addiction you*. This is how the disease grows.

But for those addicted or not, the gut-level response is often, "Bull! You are choosing to drink or snort or gamble! How is that *a disease?*"

In fact, there is incontrovertible evidence that addiction does change the brain. SPECT, PET and MRI[1] scans show specific changes to areas of the brain that result from alcohol or drug abuse or behavioral addictions. Addiction truly is a "brain disease." We also know that addiction is hereditary and there is evidence that there are specific gene "switches" triggered in addiction. But never forget! *This is a disease over which you have control, as long as you remain abstinent.* So don't let your addiction try telling you that "disease" means you have limited personal responsibility in managing your condition.

As stressed earlier, there are no excuses. No matter how strong the grip of addiction, counter measures can *always* be implemented to weaken and reverse the disease and put it into remission.

So the question becomes, what power do we have, as individuals, to escape addiction's grip? We have all of the power! In fact, the person with addiction does have control over whether he injects a substance, stops at the bar, or spends her

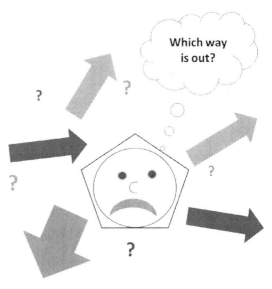

---

1 SPECT: Single photon emission computed tomography. MRI: magnetic resonance imaging. PET: positron emission tomography.

paycheck gambling. He does not have to rely on magic or the discovery of an addiction vaccine. All he or she needs is the willingness to commit to recovery and recovery-oriented actions as an unconditional, first priority.

Open-mindedness and commitment to recovery means you utilize education on the disease of addiction and develop coping skills to quash those urges and cravings. You utilize recovery resources like 12-step programs and sober friends. You work at learning to identify your using triggers and avoid situations and circumstances that threaten your abstinence. You begin to think and behave in new ways.

And the foundation for being able to do all of these things is possessing the healthy mind and body that comes from a regular program of exercise and healthy nutritional choices.

The irony is that once a person understands that she does not have control over the substance or addictive behavior, she gains control. That is not to say recovery is easy from here-on-out. But people with substance-use disorders or behavioral addictions *do* have control over the progress or remission of the disease. You either keep using. Or you stop using.

It's your choice. You know and I know that if you want to keep drinking and using, or live a life of relapse punctuated by periods of abstinence, you will. No one or thing can stop you.

And if you chose to make abstinence an unconditional tenet of your life, you can do that, instead. For the addict, there is no in-between. No gray areas. You're either living a recovery lifestyle or you're not.

I tell my clients that stopping substance or behavioral addictions is the easy part. Staying stopped is the trick.

This book outlines principles and motivation for staying stopped for good.

2

Roots of Addiction

How Addictions Begin

How do our behaviors become increasingly wedded to acting in ways that are detrimental to our health and happiness? Most people who enter treatment or find themselves in 12-step meetings started their patterns of use as adolescents or young adults, though older people (ages 40 and up) find themselves increasingly at risk for substance use disorders. People who start their "recreational" drug use as teens are about 50 percent more likely to develop an addiction problem than those who started their use later in life. However, we also have an aging population comfortable with our "take a pill to fix it" culture. These people are increasingly at risk as they run head-long into the challenges of getting older.

Creating Future Addicts from Adolescents

Many types of addiction, perhaps most particularly substance-abuse addictions, begin during adolescence. At first glance, it seems easy to understand why. There are obvious aspects of teen-age behavior that would seem to put them at increased risk for the use of drugs and alcohol.

✓ Adolescence is marked by anxiety, changes in sleep rhythms, increased novelty and risk-taking behavior, diminished awareness of danger, and emotional and temperament changes.

✓ Adolescents seek new identities, ones with greater autonomy and independence from family. This identity-seeking is further influenced by a variety of social factors. Among these are graduation from middle school to high school. In this transition, the teen often finds himself in a new and much larger social environment. He desires acceptance by peer groups and finds new interest in romantic or intimate relationships.

We are familiar with the physical changes — sexual maturation and increase in height and weight — that take place from age 12 to 18. But there are other changes that take place inside the brain that we cannot see.

The teen brain undergoes numerous structural, chemical, developmental and environmental changes in adolescence. Some of these continue until as late as the age of 25. The biological impact of drugs and alcohol on the developing adolescent brain makes it more difficult for the teen to make sound decisions, and alters the way the brain wires itself. (1) Adolescents engaging in regular use of psychoactive chemicals face adverse impacts on their biopsychosocial (biological, psychological and social) development, often with permanent consequences. (2) Here are two real life examples of what I am talking about.

Charlie was a 16-year old boy from a broken family and suffered severe socio-economic distress. His father had never been part of his life. His mother was addicted to drugs.

Ever since Charlie could remember, he took responsibility for caring for his two younger siblings, cooking and trying to get them to school. His mother had lots of "company" and Charlie had his first experiences with alcohol at age nine, when he would drink what was left in the cups after Mom's parties.

Charlie began smoking marijuana shortly thereafter; in fact, he simply followed his mother's example. There was always leftover booze and weed around, and he also would steal from her stash when she was passed out.

Charlie's addiction grew to include prescription pain-killers and heroin. When Charlie arrived in treatment, he had been referred by the criminal justice system after participating in the armed robbery of a pizza-delivery driver.

What was remarkable about Charlie was the fact that he appeared to be approximately 12 years of age. He was physically under-developed for a teenage boy of 16. Not surprisingly, Charlie had not performed well in school; his thinking ability and behavioral deficits placed him at approximately third-grade level. When he went to the gym with my group, he demonstrated relatively poor motor skills in simply throwing and catching a ball. Clearly, drug use had resulted in physical, cognitive (thinking and learning) and social (behavioral) deficits.

Jamie was a 17-year-old girl from an upper middle-class family. She had everything she wanted in the form of material possessions. She was also bright, a good athlete and a very attractive young lady. Her experiences using drugs started with drinking and were related to "wanting to fit in" experimentation, and "having fun."

She also felt "she deserved" a reward for her "hard work and achievements."

During her early individual counseling sessions, Jamie repeatedly insisted that she felt she was missing the attention and love of her parents. (Note the classic defense mechanism here of blaming: "It's not my fault I'm using drugs, it's my parents' fault.")

"Them buying me a Jeep for my 16th birthday is just a way for them to feel better about never being here for me." (Jamie's parents were classic dual executives with much job-related travel. Once again, however, we all know many people who have suffered feelings of abandonment, trauma and other countless horrors, but do not become drug addicts or alcoholics.)

Jamie finally got her parents attention: her addiction progressed to injecting heroin in her bedroom, purposely leaving the door open. Unfortunately, she was the one who paid the price. By the time she went to treatment, her addiction had come to color her behaviors and belief systems. She lost her full-ride scholarship to college. Her parents' behavior, on the other hand, did not change.

But her brain certainly had. And although she had the potential to recover physically and psychologically, Jamie wasn't 18 yet and had already suffered what many substance abusers fail to consider: the opportunities forever lost because of addiction.

We tend to focus on the most catastrophic consequences of addiction: potential car crashes, disease and possible financial ruin. But what about failing to visit a grandparent during her last days? Or missing your child's first birthday?

Or failing to perform at an important job interview? Or losing that college scholarship?

Creating Addicts from Temperate Adults

Now that I've addressed some of the issues with younger people, what about adult-onset addictions, especially those that might
begin in mid-life? Well, the process isn't much different from what
happens in adolescents, except that — generally speaking — physical, occupational and social consequences can occur more rapidly
than they do in the younger person.

Although the brain is fully developed in the middle-aged
or older adult, the process of aging has begun to have both
subtle and overt effects on the older adult's metabolism. So not
only is the adult or geriatric adult at risk based upon the addictive properties of psychoactive substances she might use, but
her body is simply not as efficient at processing and eliminating
toxins.

Furthermore, the older adult (especially over 65) has frequently suffered grief and loss issues with family, friends and sometimes
children. Loneliness and poor health can cause older adults to
self-medicate. Bad marriages and social relationships can also be
triggers, including those that are "co-dependent" or toxic.

Additionally, the older adult is more likely to have other diseases or conditions, such as cardiovascular disease, diabetes, obesity, stress-related illnesses, cancer and cognitive or brain disorders
such as dementia or Parkinson's disease. Because of this, addictive behaviors may progress more rapidly to an acute state in older
adults than they do adolescents or young adults. And they do so
because the older adult is both less resilient and more vulnerable
to the effects of psychoactive substances.

Mary was a 58-year-old nurse. She was married to an alcoholic, but never really enjoyed drinking, other than a glass of wine with dinner or at the infrequent special occasion. Her alcoholic husband was in denial, and she had been actively enabling him for the last 20 years.

Two years ago, while caring for her terminally ill mother, Mary's back was killing her and she was simply "beat" as she recalled. "I took one of my Mom's pills and, boy, was that a relief! My back felt better, I had more energy to care for Mom and I wasn't as pissed off at Henry when I got home and found him perched in his chair with the TV blaring."

As a nurse, Mary knew the potential consequences of her actions. On the other hand, the stress of her circumstances had become too much. Rather than asking for help, or dealing with her toxic relationship, taking pills was the easiest way to deal with her responsibilities. No confrontations, no conflict.

Unfortunately, Mary's use quickly became abuse and dependence. When her mother passed, she continued using. She had begun to believe that she was "owed" something (relief) for her trials with her mother. She also felt that her husband "has his booze, why can't I have my thing?" She was admitted to detox and treatment when the hospital at which she worked caught her stealing patients' pain meds.

"I can't believe how quickly I came to need those pills every day!" Mary said. I still can't believe I was stealing from patients and putting my career and pension on the line. I'm so ashamed and feel so guilty. How could I have done this?"

So, if you start using drugs as an adolescent, you have a higher risk of developing an addiction problem because while the brain is still growing, it is simultaneously being reprogrammed by psychoactive chemicals. The older adult is prone to addiction, where no problem had previously existed, because of the effects of aging, metabolic changes, and the accumulation of life-stressors.

Let's begin to better understand how these addictions physiologically effect the brain.

The Brain and Addiction: A Quick Overview

Addictions occur as substances (alcohol/drugs) or activities (gambling, shopping, internet use, sex) impact chemical messengers in the brain. These chemical messengers then affect certain parts of the brain that are responsible for various ways that we think and behave. This thinking and behavior then become dysfunctional, resulting in what we call an addiction.

Let's take a closer look at each of these key parts of the process.

The Chemical Messengers

Neurotransmitters: These are the chemical substances that stimulate the sending of electrical signals from one brain cell (neuron) to another. Those signals result in our actions, feelings, moods and all the other things our brain governs. For the purposes of this book, there are two key things to know about them.

- ✓ They have a big influence on our moods. They can make us feel good, or they can make us feel bad.
- ✓ We become addicted, in part, because alcohol, drugs, sex and other substances and activities can raise or lower the levels of these neurotransmitters in our brains. In future chapters, we will see how exercise and diet can combat addictions by doing the exact same thing: increasing or

decreasing these neurotransmitters, but in a healthy and productive way.

Dopamine: This governs reward, pleasure and motivation. Dopamine effectively tells us to repeat that behavior, do it again, and do more. Excess dopamine is a side effect in people who have used substances like cocaine (or crack) or methamphetamine (speed, ice).

Binges — several days or weeks of non-stop use — result in paranoia, formication (feeling of bugs crawling on or under the skin), delusions (black helicopters and the FBI are watching) or hallucination (seeing, hearing or smelling something not there).

The body can also naturally have too much or too little dopamine. Too much dopamine is thought to cause psychotic symptoms and thought disorders such as those experienced by schizophrenics (auditory hallucinations, feelings of paranoia, etc.). Too little dopamine is implicated in Parkinson's disease and other muscle movement or control disorders.

Endorphins and Enkephalins: Drugs like prescription painkillers – OxyContin®, Roxicet®, Percocet®, Lortab®, Vicodin®, Methadone® – and heroin are opiates. They not only reduce or eliminate pain, they can make us feel good, even euphoric. Endorphins and enkephalins are the body's natural opiates. They reduce pain and elevate mood. They help govern our emotional reactions when we are injured. And they produce the "runner's high" that runners and all kinds of athletes feel after (and during) the exertion of physical activity. They also play key roles in other important brain functions. Beta-endorphin, for example, supports the brain's ability to correct errors and modulate our emotional-behavioral responses. It also affects how efficiently we think. (3)

Serotonin: This is a mood regulator. It is also critical in regulating body temperature. People with depression are typically assumed to have too little serotonin. Common anti-depressants are designed to control some of the reabsorption of naturally-occurring serotonin so the depressed person has a more "normal" level. Most psychoactive drugs increase the amount of serotonin available in the brain. MDMA/Ecstasy/Molly is a drug that heavily increases the amount of serotonin in the brain, often resulting in hyperthermia (excessive body temperature) and extreme listlessness and depression after "coming down." Dysfunctional serotonin levels are also associated with obsessions and compulsions.

Norepinephrine and epinephrine: These are produced in the adrenal glands and are our natural stimulants. They govern the "fight or flight response" that makes us want to either run away from threatening situations or make a stand and fight. They also promote concentration and alertness. Stimulant drugs such as cocaine, methamphetamine and Ritalin/Adderall (methylphenidate) increase the amount of these in the bloodstream and available to the brain.

GABA: This stands for gamma-amino butyric acid. This neurotransmitter is an "inhibitory" chemical and is associated with a calming effect. In other words, it is like a natural Valium®, Xanax®, or Ativan®, which are benzodiazepines. In alcohol and benzodiazepine abuse, the brain starts producing less GABA in an effort to counterbalance the drugs being taken. So when the user stops drinking or taking these pills, his natural production of GABA is low. The result leaves him with familiar withdrawal feelings of anxiety, stress, and panic, and can result in seizures or death.

Glutamate: This is an excitatory neurotransmitter. It fires an electrical signal that activates another nerve cell in the brain, or a muscle or gland. In alcoholics (or abusers of other drugs that depress the central nervous system) the brain creates more gluta-mate than it should and less GABA than it should – all in an effort to balance out the effects of the alcohol, benzodiazepines, or other depressant drugs. All that extra glutamate causes an excess of elec-trical signal firing and, along with a GABA deficit, can result in seizure and death without professional medical detoxification.

Anandamide: This is the body's version of cannabinoids, which are things like marijuana and hashish. Anandamide binds to the same receptors in the brain that cannabinoids do. Anandamide is thought to affect mood, reinforcement and reward. The endocan-nabinoid system affects movement and homeostasis (balance, or stability, of body systems and reactions).

Chemical Messengers and Addiction

Researchers Darryl Inaba and William Cohen have called these neurotransmitters our "happy messengers." (4). They make us FEEL GOOD. And/or they allow us not to feel things we don't want to feel.

We can use illegal and prescription drugs, and gambling and certain other activities to stimulate these chemical messengers and feel virtually any way we want to feel. Stressed? Take a Xanax®. Too tired to study? Snort some coke or pop an Adderall®. Can't stand the pain of a relationship breakup? Drink some booze or smoke some heroin to numb the pain. Want to "be chill" and re-lax? Smoke a joint.

Drugs and behavioral addictions are the escape hatch through which we avoid reality precisely because of how they stimulate the cascade of these "happy messengers."

And it's not just the substance or activity that produces this effect. Just *thinking* about these substances can stimulate our neurotransmitters, although not as long or as well as actually taking the substance. That's why we feel good when we are at the liquor store check-out counter, or getting drugs from the pharmacy or drug dealer.

Think about it. You were already feeling high before ingesting the substance, or laying down the first bet, right? Now you know why. The "happy messengers" are stimulated by the *anticipation* of using the drug. Which is exactly what euphoric recall is. A form of anticipation. And why counselors discourage all story-telling and reminiscing about "the good old days" of using. Euphoric recall is a trap that feeds cravings.....and relapse.

Now what the heck are these neurotransmitters doing in the brain, where do they go and why is it so hard to "just stop" our addictions?

3

How Addiction Changes the Brain

To better understand how the brain becomes re-wired to addiction and why we end up behaving the way we do as addicts, alcoholics, problem gamblers, etc., we need to learn more about the brain itself.

Brain Basics 101

Neurons are a type of brain cell. They transmit messages, chemically or electrically, to produce thoughts, actions and other brain functions.

Neurons are composed of a cell body, an axon and dendrites. The axon looks like a long cable and the dendrites look like roots of a plant. The dendrites receive message(s) from other brain cells; the axon transmits those messages to other brain cells. The messages (neurotransmitters) travel across an extremely small gap — called a **synapse** — between neurons.

Illegal and legal drugs, and alcohol affect us by fitting into **receptor** sites on the neurons. These receptor sites are like locks, and the drugs are like keys. Heroin, as one example, fits like a "key" into a mu opioid receptor "lock."

Cocaine, for instance, fills different receptors and blocks the neuron's ability to reabsorb dopamine. As a result, excess dopamine builds up in the synapse. This makes the dopamine-related reward/ motivation "circuits" (more on this in the next sections) fire excessively. I become euphoric and energized. This might seem like a good thing, but it's not. Over the course of our substance-abuse and dependence, our brains try to maintain the proper balance of dopamine and other neurotransmitters by increasing or decreasing the number of receptor sites. The end result is to create greater and greater tolerance to the drug. Our brains become re-wired to addiction.

Understand different keys may fit the same lock. That's how anti-craving drugs can counteract the effects of street or other drugs of abuse. For example, the drug given in the event of heroin overdose, naloxone, (Narcan®), is better at fitting the mu-opioid receptor than heroin is. So the naloxone key goes into the lock and blocks the heroin key. Boom. Overdose stops and withdrawal starts.

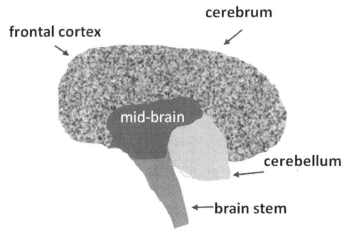

←Front   SIDE VIEW   Back →

Major Brain Components

The **brain stem**, the most primitive area of the brain, is directly connected to the spinal cord. It is responsible for breathing, heart rate, digestion, body temperature, and other essential, involuntary life functions. Deaths from heroin, alcohol and other depressants occur because overdoses of these substances put the brain stem to sleep. The signals that tell the lungs to breathe are turned off. So we stop breathing, which results in asphyxia (suffocation) and heart attack.

The **cerebrum** is the largest part of the brain. It's essentially what we see when we imagine a picture of the brain. The cerebrum is the most recent part of the brain to evolve. It integrates the "higher" functions of thought, judgment, and reason with our emotions, voluntary movements, learning, memory and personality.

The **frontal cortex** is part of the cerebrum. It is responsible for reason, judgment, planning, and the ability to delay gratification and thwart impulsiveness. The first place psychoactive substances impact the brain is in these higher-level, executive functions.

For those who have sworn off their drug of choice, only to end up relapsing after drinking a couple of beers, this is the answer to your question of "But how could this have happened?" Any psychoactive substance first affects the user's judgment and casts away inhibition. I like to tell my groups that using psychoactive substances is like giving the "boss" a sleeping pill. When no one is in charge, our base impulses and desires run the show.

As noted earlier, frontal cortex is not fully developed until approximately age 25. That's part of the reason that adolescents and children behave like, well, adolescents and children.

The Mid-Brain Area: Home of Addiction

There are complex chemical reasons why we continue to use psychoactive substances despite the various adverse consequences we suffer along the way. Part of the reason is this: we are motivated to get more and do more because our brains have come to find greater reward and immediate satisfaction in using drugs than in not using them. So we keep using them. And by doing so, we keep a more primitive part of our brain in charge. Let's look at why and how this happens.

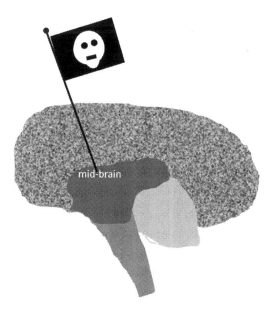

The **limbic system** is home to several integrated brain structures that are really central to addiction. When you are addicted to something, *this is where that addiction really "lives."*

The **amygdala** is the part of the limbic system responsible for emotion and fear (fight, flight, or freeze) and/or self-preservation responses such as disgust, avoidance, defensiveness, anger and aggression.

The **hippocampus** is involved in processing and recording memories and the emotions tied to those memories. This structure is also involved in conscious learning, such as learning the material in this book or what you were taught in treatment or at AA meetings, etc.

Abuse becomes addiction because our repeated use marries drug-taking to the *survival instincts* that the limbic system governs. Think about how you reacted when someone threatened to cut off your drug supply or demanded you stop drinking or gambling. Did you feel like a cornered rat? I did. Anger, fear, extreme anxiety, depression, the impulse to run or lash out at the "attacker," crying and negotiating are some of the addicted person's reactions to the threat of having to stop.

The **striatum** is located in the same mid-brain area as the limbic system. It is integrated with the **basal ganglia**. These structures play a role in addiction because of how we perceive and process stimuli, how we set goals, perceive reward (and repeat behaviors because of the perceived benefit) and are motivated.

The striatum plays a role in motor functions and in cognitive functions, including learning habits. The neurotransmitter dopamine plays a large role in how this area of the brain functions and how motivation and goal-seeking are impacted. (5) There is also evidence that this area of the brain is involved in creating reward pathways.

What is a pathway? An electrical circuit. The neurotransmitters and neurons "wire-up" brain structures, such as the **nucleus accumbens**, because of its role in our seeking reward and pleasure. Repetitive firing increases the strength of that circuit.

Other addiction-related structures included in this wiring process include the **orbitofrontal cortex**, which helps to determine the value of a potential reward, and the **subcallosal area,** which is associated with perceiving pleasure.

Please don't think you need to memorize all of this in order to get or stay clean. I have clients who are fascinated by how the pieces of the puzzle fit together. Others, not so much.

What's important is that you simply get a sense of what this stuff is and how it works. Why? Because it's integral to understanding why addiction is a brain disease. And how exercise and proper nutrition can rebalance your brain.

How the Addiction Electrician Rewires Our Brains

There are four major circuits involved in addiction (5). Understand that any brain "circuit" is reinforced by repetitive use. That means that "neurons that fire together, wire together." By the way, I can't take credit for that nifty quote. I've read it in many journals and books. It sure conveys a memorable image.

An analogy I use in groups describes a grass field that sits between the gymnasium and parking lot at the community center. There is a concrete walkway, but everyone cuts across the lawn to get to their cars. You've all seen this. The more folks traipse across the grass, the deeper the rut in the lawn becomes. Pretty soon, it's as if no one can see the concrete pathway any longer. And now *everyone* uses the dirt path in the lawn. Automatically. Without thinking.

Reward and Salience Circuit

When we take drugs, drink alcohol or do certain risky behaviors, we feel rewarded. Reward, of course, means a positive benefit to me. My reward in taking drugs is feeling less pain. Or feeling happy, or forgetting my problems, etc. Salience means that something stands out to me as being important. And needed.

So reward and salience means my need for drugs is tied to my experience that I will find great euphoria/relief/benefit in using them.

Dopamine plays an extraordinary role here. Now it is released *even when I anticipate the reward* that comes from doing an addictive behavior. This is precisely why a person feels "high" or happy *before* a drug enters his system, or *before* he lays down that first bet.

Recall that increasing the levels of dopamine in the brain fuels goal-directed behavior. And with drugs our goals are hijacked. Addiction-oriented goals such as "get more drugs" or "go back to the casino" crowd out healthy goals such as getting to work on time or taking the kids to the zoo.

Inhibition, Executive Decision-Making and Control Circuit

These functions are associated with the frontal cortex and a nearby structure, the **anterior cingulate gyrus**. As previously discussed, the former is responsible for executive functions such as decision-making, rational thinking, planning, and thwarting impulsivity. Cognition and personality are located in this area. The anterior cingulate gyrus "coordinates sensory input with emotions; regulates emotional responses to pain and regulates aggressive behavior." (6)

Psychoactive drugs limit the functioning of the frontal cortex and the anterior cingulate gyrus. This reduces our inhibition of emotions and reaction, and lessens our ability to anticipate future consequences. We become less adept at thinking. Our personalities are often changed. For the adolescent or young adult, whose frontal cortex has yet to fully develop, this is a big problem.

For example, the college frat boy takes the bet that he can't jump off the 3rd story balcony and land in the apartment pool below, rather than on the concrete decking. Or the adolescent girl plans to hook-up with a stranger she "met" on the internet for some free weed.

But it's also a big problem for the mature adult.

Let's say I get into an argument with my husband, storm out of the house and jump into my car. "I'll show him!" Suddenly, driving 90 mph, weaving in and out of traffic on my way to the drug dealer's house seems like a "solution." I'm not bothered by any consideration of all of the things that can go terribly wrong. And this is not how I used to handle confrontation before I started using drugs.

The role of alcohol has been studied in regard to this addiction circuit. Experiments on chronic alcohol exposure have found brain-cell degeneration and reduced decision-making ability in humans and rats. The subjects, whether humans or rats, were more likely to accept short-term rewards, instead of delaying gratification for a larger reward later.

This circuit of addiction, then, makes us much more vulnerable to the short-term rewards of addictive behaviors. Is it any wonder why it's hard to see the potential future benefits of recovery, versus giving in to the impulse to go out drinking again with my buddies?

Learning and Memory Circuit

We've seen how addictive substances or behaviors create reward pathways in the brain. As we continue to use these substances or do these behaviors, a neurochemical cascade essentially tells the brain to "keep doing it." The brain (and body) become habituated (used to) these chemical cascades.

This "need for more" resides in the limbic system, the home of the amygdala and hippocampus. You'll recall that both of these areas are associated with emotion, learning and memory.

The **amygdala** is also associated with "conditioned responses." Remember how I said we can already feel high when we get money to buy alcohol at the liquor store, or drugs from our drug dealer? This is a conditioned response. Like Pavlov's bell-ringing elicited drooling by his dogs in anticipation of being fed.

This conditioned response is reinforced in ritual. A ritual for a heroin addict might be getting the drug, cooking it, drawing it into a syringe and shooting it. For an alcoholic it could be getting off work at the plant and starting the drive to Mo's Tavern for happy hour. These rituals become the way we learn and reinforce addictions, and they can be as powerful as the addictions themselves. We have powerful emotional memories tied to these actions, which is why it is so difficult to resist our triggers[2].

The **hippocampus** is responsible for processing the short-term memories and the emotions associated with them. In something called "flash bulb memory," (5) extreme personal experiences are recorded and later transferred to long-term memory. Thirteen years on, no doubt everyone can remember with precise detail where they were and what was going on around them when they heard about the first plane hitting the World Trade Center. That is "flash-bulb" memory.

When an experience is particularly awesome, or pleasurable, our memory of it can make us try to repeat it – even when those repetitions don't make us feel nearly as good any more. Drug users call this "chasing the dragon." They remember that first time (or first few times) when the high of using a drug was incomparable.

---

2 Activities, people, places, things, and patterns of thinking that provoke urges, cravings and potentially relapse.

Even though subsequent use is never quite as pleasurable, the intense memory of that unbelievable first high drives them to keep using and using and using and…

Another important thing to remember about the limbic system is that it is tied in to primitive emotions and survival instincts, like fear, anger and the "fight or flight" response. Abuse becomes dependence (addiction) because our repeated use marries drug-taking to the survival instincts that the limbic system governs. Think again about how you reacted when someone threatened to cut off your supply, or demanded you stop drinking or gambling. The extreme emotional responses, the anger, the fear, you felt derive from this system.

Motivation and Drive Circuit

Why do we continue to use psychoactive substances despite the various adverse consequences we suffer along the way? Part of the reason is this: we are motivated to get more and do more because our brains have come to find greater reward and immediate satisfaction in doing drugs than in stopping. So we keep doing them. And by doing so we keep the more primitive parts of our brains in charge.

Everything we do now is driven by our need to use and our desire to get more. We are driven by our addiction and motivated not just to feel good, but to *not* feel bad. How is this cycle perpetuated?

When we anticipate doing something that will give us a reward, our anticipation sets off the release of the neurotransmitter dopamine. The drug then prompts the release of more neurotransmitters, which produce the physiological "high" as well as the other mental and physical responses.

For instance, taking cocaine "blocks the reuptake of dopamine, norepinephrine and serotonin, thereby forcing these neurotransmitters to react longer." (7) The result is euphoria, energy and confidence. In addition, we have heightened fight-or-flight responses, including such effects as increased heart rate, blood pressure, alertness, and pupil dilation.

But an unwanted side effect of repeating this process is unpleasant feelings (as the drugs wear off or become less effective because of the tolerance we have built to the substance) such as unhappiness, anxiety, agitation and depression. To relieve these feelings, the brain seeks more drugs, which, in turn, release more neurotransmitters. This cycle of using is incredibly difficult to stop and becomes even harder the longer the addiction goes unchecked.

This is because the brain also seeks to maintain balance, or homeostasis. For instance, as its dopamine levels rise, the brain begins to reduce the number of available dopamine receptors. This creates increased tolerance to the effects of the drug. I need more and more to even come close to feeling a good or satisfying high. The cycle of addiction is in full swing. Note that, in some people, this process is so strong that the individual can become psychologically dependent with only one or a few uses.

Tying it all together

Let's sum up.

- ✓ Psychoactive substances and certain behaviors feed a reward pathway, resulting in the stimulation of the "happy messengers" (brain chemicals) known to elevate mood, relieve anxiety, and promote a sense of well-being and happiness.
- ✓ The intense good feelings we get from addictive behaviors interfere with our ability to make good decisions and control our impulses and emotions. This makes us

even more susceptible to the short-term rewards of these behaviors, at the expense of our long-term health and happiness.

✓ Repeated use of the substance or behavior creates a neuro-chemical cascade that essentially tells our brains to "keep doing it." This "need" for more resides in the limbic system, the location of the amygdala and hippocampus. This area retains memories of pleasurable experiences and rituals associated with the addictive activity. These become highs in themselves, and condition us to keep doing the activity. The limbic system is also home to primitive emotions that make the drug user, gambler, or alcoholic terrified of giving up their addictive activity, and act as if their lives depended upon doing more of it.

✓ Our brains and bodies become habituated to the chemical cascades produced by addictive activities. Without them we feel sick, shaky, angry, anxious and depressed. This makes us need these activities even more, and drives us to do them again.

One is too many and a thousand is never enough." — AA saying.

Hopefully, you're beginning to understand why stopping drug, alcohol and process addictions is so difficult. The deviant behaviors, the destruction of our lives, and loss of our souls, is not a moral failing. It's a result of a brain disease with genetic, hereditary and environmental underpinnings.

This also means that it's a repairable problem that is predictable in both its course of destruction and its path to long-term remission. Stopping (and staying stopped) is not beyond your control. It simply means that it is hard work and you need to put the kind of energy into staying stopped that you did into developing and maintaining your addiction.

We know how to fix this. You *can* get better, but you must be willing to give 100 percent effort.

"Half-measures availed us nothing…" – AA's Big Book

4

How Exercise Promotes Recovery and Prevents Relapse

A Trick to Staying Stopped?

What if I told you there was a healthy and inexpensive way to heal body and mind from the ravages of addiction? What if I further told you that this same approach would help keep you addiction-free over the long term?

Crazy, right?

Wrong! Exercise can fundamentally and significantly decrease the severity of the unpleasant physical, psychological, social and spiritual symptoms felt during early recovery. Furthermore, a continuing program of exercise will help to prevent relapse. In fact, exercise fits hand-in-glove with both clinical and 12-step (or other abstinence-based) programs of recovery. We will see how later in this chapter.

Remember our discussion of how addiction produces an imbalance of brain neurotransmitters? A regular fitness program can repair the brain, grow new brain cells and help prevent relapse. And you don't have to become an Olympic athlete, or even a gym rat. Scientific findings and my clinical and personal experiences demonstrate that there is great benefit for anyone willing to exercise regularly.

Exercise encourages the relatively quick return of the brain's proper balance of neurotransmitters and receptor sites. When you exercise, you use your body to heal your mind, and defeat your addiction.

In a nutshell, here is what happens. Exercise:

✓ Helps puts your brain chemicals back into homeostasis, or balance. Exercise actually promotes the growth of new neurons in the limbic system.
✓ Helps you stay healthier, and heal faster when you are sick or injured.
✓ Stimulates and rebalances your "happy" neurotransmitters. This relieves depression, stress and anxiety. It enhances mood, self-esteem and confidence.
✓ Exercise can help you change your life for the better, reduce your loneliness and isolation, and make you a happier, more socially-involved person.
✓ Exercise puts you in better touch with your body and improves your self image. It can contribute to meditation, mindfulness and spirituality.

"Sobriety is a journey, not a destination." — AA Saying

And so it is with exercise and nutrition.

Post-Acute Withdrawal Symptoms (PAWs)

Those of you who have not been in treatment might not know what PAWs is. Those of you who have been in treatment might not remember! PAWs is the first hurdle people face in recovery. It's the challenge that keeps a lot of people addicted because it seems so hard to get over.

One of the most crucial ways that exercise helps recovering addicts is in reducing the effects of PAWs.

Post-acute withdrawal is a cluster of symptoms that begin after the acute withdrawal period has ended. You end up with these symptoms as a result of how your brain and body changed to deal with your drug use or behavior patterns. When we take away those drugs/activities, your brain is out-of-balance — at least until it has a chance to get rebalanced.

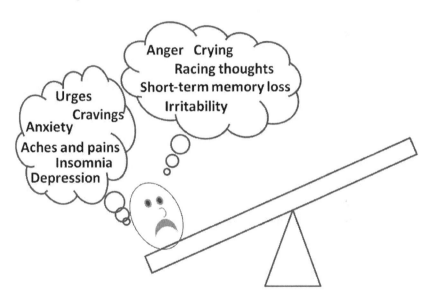

**Post-Acute
Withdrawal**

Before going further, let's define what acute withdrawal is.

Acute withdrawal symptoms are more severe and include vomiting, diarrhea, severe shaking, severe anxiety, wracking body aches and pains, hallucinations, seizure and possibly death if not treated medically. Most people do not know that, while opiate (heroin, pain pills like Oxycodone®, Percocet® and Vicodin®, etc.) withdrawal can be particularly nasty, it is not fatal. However, acute alcohol and/or benzodiazepine (Valium®, Xanax®, Ativan®, etc.) withdrawal, left untreated, can result in seizure and death. The acute withdrawal period is NOT the time to do anything other than seek medical treatment.

The post-acute withdrawal symptoms (PAWs) period begins after detoxification has ended, typically five to seven days after last use, but it can be longer depending upon the degree to which addiction has altered your brain and damaged your body.

The severity and duration of PAWs also depends on the following:

- ✓ How long you have used and the intensity with which you have used. If you've used every day for several years, PAWS can be worse than for someone who has used for 10 years, but not as often.
- ✓ Your age. The older you are, the more difficult you may find PAWs.
- ✓ Which drug or drug combinations you have used.
- ✓ Whether you have an underlying or co-occurring mental health disorder like depression, bi-polar disorder, post-traumatic stress disorder, etc.
- ✓ Whether you have other medical conditions or chronic disease.

PAWs may last up to two years! My clinical experience indicates that PAWs lasts anywhere from three months to 18 months. My personal experience was that PAWs lasted approximately eight to 10 months. That might seem like a long time, but the symptoms gradually dissipate over that period. In my case, eight to 10 months was how long it took until the last physical, cognitive and emotional symptoms faded away.

PAWs Affect Those in Recovery in the Following Ways:

Cognitive (thinking): These include the inability to think clearly, short-term memory problems, inability to focus or complete a thought, and difficulties with abstract thinking and solving problems.

Coordination: Problems with balance, hand-eye coordination, gait and posture.

General Physical: Nausea, sleeplessness, restlessness, lack of appetite or over-eating, aches and pains, anxiety and agitation.

Emotional problems: Over-reaction to stress, emotional numbness, emotional volatility, depression, mood swings, dichotomous (all-or-nothing, or black-and-white) thinking, excessive feelings of shame and guilt, angry outbursts and racing thoughts.

I'm going to present both scientific and anecdotal evidence on precisely how exercise promotes elimination of the PAW symptoms. We'll also learn specifically how exercise reinforces the biological, psychological, social and spiritual healing necessary to recover from addiction.

Too Good and Easy to be True?

No. And here is some research evidence to back up what I have personally experienced, as well as witnessed in counseling and training my clients.

Alcohol and Exercise

In research on alcoholic patients, those engaging in aerobic and strength-training exercise experienced lower levels of depression and anxiety than those in the control group. Patients in the exercise group also more readily developed coping skills and displayed better tolerance to stress. (13)

Nicotine and Behavioral Addiction

In nine of 10 studies reviewed by Scerbo, Faulkner, Taylor, and Thomas (14) exercise reduced nicotine cravings and withdrawal symptoms in those who participated. Symptoms improved through exercise included "…anxiety, stress, tension, poor concentration, irritability, and restlessness." (p11).

Studies indicate that smokers have 36% higher cortisol concentrations than those of non-smokers. Cortisol is the stress hormone that helps us in many ways, from coping with threats to simply waking up in the morning. It helps get us moving. However, high levels of cortisol have been associated with smaller hippocampus volume (3). Excessive amounts of cortisol are also associated with diabetes, obesity, sugar cravings and immune-system suppression.

Cocaine and Opiates

Studies of rats have shown that exercise can reduce the need for opiate drugs. Rats running on a wheel displayed reduced cravings for cocaine (14). Studies of rats running on treadmills indicated that short and moderate-term exercise could lower the animals' need for morphine (15).

The researchers in these studies found not only an increase in dopamine in the exercising rats, but also hypothesized that higher levels of glutamate found in the rats' prefrontal cortexes protected against relapse.

Cannabis

Marijuana (cannabis) users who had no desire to quit using or seek treatment reduced their use after two weeks of running on a treadmill. When they stopped exercising, their cannabis use returned to the original levels (16).

The researchers also studied cravings during the experimental period using the Marijuana Craving Questionnaire. They found statistical significance in a reduction in cravings between pre-exercise and post-exercise period assessments.

It's plausible that exercise not only reduces cravings and withdrawal symptoms in marijuana users by stimulating "feel good" neurotransmitters such as endorphin and dopamine, but also helps to replace "lost" marijuana by stimulating our natural cannabinoids. A University of Arizona study (11) found that exercise increased endocannabinoid levels among people who ran on treadmills for 30 minutes at about four miles per hour, or about the speed it takes to run a mile in 17.5 minutes.

Multiple Substance Dependence

Exercise can reduce the need for drugs among those with polysubstance abuse (abusing more than one drug). A study of 43 female adolescents found that exercise reduced their polysubstance abuse. The young women also improved their physical fitness, as well as "overall feelings of well-being, self-esteem, healthy lifestyle adoption, health awareness and relapse prevention skills." (17) (p. 87)

Let's understand how this will work for you, in your life!

Retrofitting Our Damaged Brains

You've learned that addiction "lives" in the limbic system. Believe it or not, exercise has been shown to grow new brain cells (neurogenesis) in this area of the brain, specifically in the hippocampus.

You may be thinking, "That's impossible!" I thought the same thing. How many brain scientists, and years of public service announcements(PSAs) and TV commercials have told us that "once you kill a brain cell, it's never coming back"? Many of us remember the fried egg PSAs in the 1980s – "This is your brain (an egg). This is your brain on drugs (egg frying in frying pan). Any questions?" But through modern brain-imaging technology, scientists have learned much about how drugs, exercise and disease (among other things) impact various areas of the brain – either positively or negatively. These technologies have actually allowed scientists to see parts of the brain that have either atrophied (shrunken away), grown or grown back, depending on whether they've been activated or inactivated by stimuli such as drugs.

Research indicates that exercise provides a type of stress that can stimulate neurogenesis. This stress activates production of a protein called BDNF (brain-derived neurotrophic factor).

Harvard psychiatrist John J. Ratey has called BDNF "Miracle-Gro for the brain."(11) It increases the strength of the electrical signals in the synapses between neurons. It is thought to rejuvenate neurons and promote "synaptic plasticity": the ability to increase or decrease the neurotransmitter levels when necessary by adding or subtracting receptor sites within the synapse.

What this means to us, practically-speaking, is this: the ability to grow new brain cells, protect and nurture existing brain cells, and allow brain cells to better communicate and be more adaptable. The result?

- ✓ Improves our memory and ability to learn.
- ✓ Increases levels of dopamine and serotonin.
- ✓ Improves mood, sense of well-being and self-esteem.
- ✓ Reduces depression. One study of women diagnosed with depression disorders found that their hippocampus was, on average, 15 percent smaller than women without depression. (8)

✓ Protects the dopamine neurons destroyed by Parkinson's disease. (9)

My clinical experience indicates that, for those who enter treatment facilities or who get help through 12-step or other self-help programs (or both), having an improved ability to process and store new information makes becoming open-minded and willing to work at recovery a lot easier. It also leaves that person less susceptible to going back to the old habits and thought patterns associated with using or behaving in unhealthy ways.

In fact, regular, moderate-intensity exercise has been found to have a positive, effect on our levels of dopamine, serotonin, opioid and GABA neurotransmitters.(3) Vigorous exercise – running for 15 minutes versus briskly walking for 15 minutes – has a similar effect on the anandamide system (11).

As I tell my clients, "No one here is training for the Olympics or the NFL. There are no trials or spring training deadlines looming. Take it easy, take it slow and 'keep coming back.' We are in the business of setting realistic, attainable and smart goals. And we have plenty of time in which to achieve them."

Beverly, 29, lived with her eight-week-old daughter in a women and children's residential rehab home. Her three other children, all under the age of 8, lived with her parents. She was in treatment for addiction to prescription painkillers. Beverly was also morbidly obese and smoked about a pack and a half of cigarettes per day.

Walking up the slightest inclines around the rehab house got her winded. She had a defeatist attitude when I first met her. "Exercise is not for me; I can't do it," she said. "I'm too big and I don't care."

"Well, you may not care," I replied, "but fitness group is mandatory and I need you to get in the van and come along with us. Trust me, no one is going to force you to do anything you can't do. The first step in recovery is being open-minded and willing."

Beverly grudgingly got into the van, probably more out of fear of consequences from Child Protective Services if she failed to comply with her treatment program, than for any other reason.

On her first day, she could only walk two laps around the 200-meter indoor track before she stopped from fatigue. Although the others kept going, no one laughed at her; no one judged. In fact, just the opposite. She was encouraged to do what she could and was given sincere, positive feedback for her effort. Later, she told me what she got from that first session was overcoming her fear of embarrassment at her weight and general lack of health.

After breaking the ice, and several more days of walking and increasing her distance, Beverly came to me for help. "Miss Shelley, I feel so much better about myself, getting out and trying. Now I want to do more. I want to be there for my kids. I want to be able to go with the other girls on the machines."

I took Beverly over to the elliptical machine, demonstrated how it worked and let her climb aboard. I set her initial goal at two minutes on the lowest, easiest setting. Over the next eight weeks, Beverly gradually increased her time on the elliptical, and became willing to try new exercises, including strength training. That, plus walking several laps around the track was enough of a workout for her. She also began taking on a team-leader role, helping round up the clients and gather and return all of the gym equipment at the end of group sessions.

In fact, she did not lose any weight during that time. However, what exercise instilled in Beverly was hope, an increased level of self-esteem, and the motivation to cut back on her smoking. Her primary counselor noticed that she began to take on more responsibilities in the house. The childcare workers noticed that she was more attentive to her daughter's needs. Beverly had become motivated: she was planning for a future outside of institutions, and putting some of her treatment work into practice.

I attributed much of this change in attitude to achieving Small Wins[SM] by setting and attaining limited but reachable goals each gym visit. This gave her a sense of accomplishment, which in turn gave her hope that she could reach other objectives and dreams. She was proud of herself for following through, and her self-esteem and self-confidence grew.

Change is Action, Not Talk

Beverly's exercise wasn't particularly vigorous. And she didn't become very fit. But she still derived an important benefit. Who isn't proud of themselves for following through and trying something different?! Especially when that change is uncomfortable. Beverly felt uncomfortable because of her health and size (physical discomfort). She felt "less than" the other women and feared derision or embarrassment (psychological discomfort).

Think about how many non-addicted, relatively healthy people refuse to take action toward change. I've had numerous discussions with co-workers and friends who knew about my struggles with weight gain...okay, it was actually obesity...in my early recovery.

Them: "Shelley, how do you manage to stay so fit and how did you lose that weight? I need to lose weight and get in better shape and I just don't know how to go about it."

I'd mention the importance of healthy diet and exercise, and that both need to be done together.

Them: "But isn't that just so hard?"

Me: "You count your calories. I don't mean to say you have to be perfect. You can scribble down estimates and notes in a book. Or there are lots of apps on smartphones which you can…."

Them: (eyes glazing over). "…Uhm, I can't do all of that."

I'd get the same response with exercise.

Me: "Make a schedule and go 3 to 4 times a week."

Them: "Gee, that seems like a lot. I don't really have the time…"

Me: "So you want things to be different, you want improvement, but you don't want to exert any effort, or deploy any discipline in getting there? How is that going to work?"

This conversation is a perfect analogy to recovery. I want to stay clean, but I don't want to have to go to meetings, or attend intensive outpatient, or call my sponsor, or stay out of bars, or…

This is why I think an exercise program lends itself so well psychologically to a program of recovery. Both involve a sense of fear of the unknown and of being challenged. Both require a commitment, which, as recently-using addicts/alcoholics or gamblers, we are not used to making. In fact, the only thing we could be consistent about was getting more drugs or losing more money. And feeling terrible.

The Rebalancing Act

Moderate-intensity exercise reignites your body's ability to produce and/or increase its natural levels of dopamine, serotonin, endorphins/enkephalins, GABA, glutamate, norepinephrine and epinephrine. This is important, because, depending upon the drugs you took, or activities you engaged in, your brain adapted itself to higher/altered levels of some or all of these neurotransmitters.

In early recovery, your brain has not quite gotten the message. It doesn't instantly adjust to the fact that you just decided to cut it off from all substances (get clean and sober). Remember, your brain used synaptic plasticity to try to counter-balance the over-load of dopamine, opioid, GABA, etc. that you were stimulating via drug use.

Happily, exercise is a natural way to help the brain rebalance itself faster. This means fewer cravings, better moods, better think-ing, reduced anxiety and depression and a greater tendency to use coping skills (or learn new ones).

Rebalancing My Mental State and Mental Health

There is a growing body of evidence that habitual exercise "is an adequate therapeutic agent for the treatment of major depres-sion, anxiety, Parkinson's disease, attention deficit disorder, schizo-phrenia, spinal cord injuries and chronic drug addiction."(9) As you will recall from the previous chapter, dopamine is thought to play a role in many of these diseases. Rats that exercised on wheels over a six-week period showed changes to dopaminergic systems and activity, and neuronal plasticity in the basal ganglia area of the brain. Remember that the basal ganglia is part of the limbic system and is related to how we respond to goal setting and reward.

Neuronal plasticity is like synaptic plasticity. Recall that plastic-ity means the ability to change in response to such stimuli as drugs or repetitive behaviors. Ironically, this plasticity helps stimulate ad-dictions by promoting the development of tolerance.

Later, repeated use of psychoactive substances and behavioral addictions makes our brains less elastic, or plastic. Exercise helps to reinvigorate plasticity through the growth of new cells and the making of new connections between cells. Engaging in new activities and skills-development effectively re-wires the brain!

This does not mean that exercise is a cure. But what it does mean is that exercise promotes many positive factors in the prevention and healing of certain diseases and conditions.

Of course, everyone is different, and individual response to exercise and disease management will vary.

Any positive benefit, however, is better than no benefit at all. And sitting on the couch eating chips and ice cream while binge-ing on Netflix® is not a proactive approach toward managing your addiction, or your health. Here's an example of how even the simplest exercise can make a difference.

Jonathon, a 32-year-old immigrant from Sudan, was admitted to treatment for alcohol dependence. Admission assessment found that he also suffered from post-traumatic stress disorder from witnessing the atrocities of genocide and experiencing relocation camps during his formative years.

Jonathan was very polite and generally had no problem following treatment protocol and house rules. But over several weeks' time, his behavior became more erratic and less coherent. One evening, after "lights out," he went "AWOL." Staff found him standing outside, about a block away. He had been there for an hour. "Voices" had told him to leave rehab! Jonathon was diagnosed with schizophrenia.

When he was cleared to come out for fitness group, I found that he enjoyed walking laps around the baseball field at the park. He walked and walked and walked and seemed genuinely happy.

I asked him what he liked about the walking – what might be motivating him? How did he feel when he was walking?

"I like it because I can think", he said. "When I am sitting still, I have too many thoughts and I cannot concentrate on anything. Too much stuff is flying around in my head. I can't stand it!

But when I'm walking, I can focus on each step. And then the thoughts come into my head one at a time. I can deal with that."

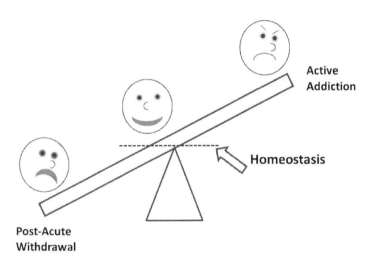

Improve Your Health. Prevent Disease.

Regular exercise has been the subject of increasing study this decade. Researchers are trying to determine how exercise and general physical fitness might prevent and/or heal various physical and psychological conditions. There is an abundance of positive causal and correlational evidence indicating that exercise and movement are useful treatments for many conditions.

The Heart: Moderate exercise promotes cardiovascular and pulmonary health by increasing the strength and efficiency of the heart muscle and lungs. Benefits include lower blood pressure and an increase in HDL cholesterol. (This is the "good" cholesterol that helps keep our blood vessel walls clean. It traps and removes bits of the "bad" cholesterol, then transports it to be reprocessed or eliminated.)

A healthy heart and circulatory system means that oxygen and nutrients travel to our brain and other organs more easily. As a result, they function better and repair themselves faster. Oxygenation and nutrient transport are critical to brain and body repair, as well as to maximizing physiological and cognitive brain function.

The Immune System: Reducing stress and tension makes our immune systems healthier. Studies have shown that people who exercise regularly and moderately produce less cortisol, the "stress" hormone. They also react less intensely to stressful situations.(19)

Diabetes: Exercise has been shown to have positive benefits for those suffering from Type II diabetes. In diabetes, exercise can lower blood sugar, increase insulin sensitivity, and aid in maintaining a healthy body weight.

Arthritis: Exercise, and specifically strength training, can help ease the symptoms of arthritis in several ways. It helps distribute synovial fluids that lubricate the joints. Exercise also builds stronger muscles, which takes some stress off the joints and reduces "wear and tear" on them.

Osteoporosis: Resistance/strength training promotes muscle and bone density and serves to prevent osteoporosis.

Creating and Maintaining Sober Living

Staying abstinent and developing a healthy lifestyle are the keys to long-term recovery. But this takes commitment and motivation. In my experience, that's where most clients fall short. Luckily, exercise can kick-start commitment and motivation.

As you've learned, exercise impacts those dopamine pathways that fuel our drive to do more. When you add regular exercise to your schedule, your brain literally becomes happier, healthier and more efficient. You are more confident and optimistic, and therefore much better able to stay motivated and committed to being a better person, finding a job, living independently, or any other recovery goal.

New People, Places and Things: Exercise is an ideal way to promote an essential recovery goal: social reintegration. Interacting with others in a positive, healthy manner. Exercise classes, team sports, or finding a workout partner or partners serves the social basis of treatment and recovery advocated by clinicians and self-help groups. This social support has the additional advantage of helping to provide positive reinforcement to continue with an exercise regimen.

You don't feel like working out this morning, but you know that Tony is looking forward to a run with you this beautiful autumn morning. So you go.

Or maybe it's too hot for softball today. But you can't leave your softball team without its 3rd baseman, can you? So you play.

Those of you already in recovery, how many times have you felt like not going to a meeting, only to think of how the folks in your home group might miss you, or worry about you? So you drag yourself out of bed and get your butt to the meeting.

This social aspect of fitness and recovery are analogous. We use the same cognitive and behavioral tools to make the necessary changes in our lives.

Drilling Down

Cognitive. *Thinking. In the examples above, I demonstrated how one changes how he thinks about exercise (or going to a meeting). Rather than* *it being an inconvenience, or "the weather is terrible, I want to stay in", or "I might be uncomfortable", we learn to restructure our thoughts. We replace the negative thinking with positive thinking. "I'm always in such a good mood when I get out of a meeting (or finish exercising)."*

Or we consider how meetings and exercise help us with relapse prevention, and support our physical and psychological health. That's not to say it might not be cold this winter morning. But we need to retrain ourselves to seek the silver lining, rather than always defaulting to the dark cloud.

***Behavioral.** Actions I take. Simple. The more frequently I do something, the more routine it becomes and the more embedded the activity (and thinking) become in my lifestyle. Repeated actions are thought to take about 90 days before they become habitual. We know what happened when we started using on a regular basis. Why not take this principle and turn it to our advantage? Exercise, like going to meetings, requires you take that first step alone, but thereafter, you never have to be alone again. Then again, what's to prevent you from asking a friend, family member or someone you met in treatment to be your "wing-man" and help support you in your first step(s) forward?*

Working with others or forming alliances serves the same purpose in establishing and maintaining a program of fitness. You might eventually self-motivate and start your own team or gym class. You might not. The point is, with the support of others, the "lifting" is easier.

So joining a gym or a team presents the opportunity to develop a broader social network of new and healthy friends (versus going back with your old drinking/drugging/gambling buddies). The fitness activities in which you engage – sports, hiking, biking, gym, etc. – undoubtedly will take you away from the old places that got you into trouble (like bars, casinos, drug houses/ neighborhoods).

The "social" aspect of exercise in addiction recovery is like being on a basketball court where you get to score on both baskets. It's win-win. A win for relapse prevention and a win for your health.

So get out there! You might be surprised by how much fun you can have, or what unknown ability you might possess!

Exercise as a Coping Skill: Health and fitness-related activities not only provide an alternative to psychoactive chemical use, but serve as a coping skill. Early recovery is an especially rough time of facing the conflicts and problems that resulted from our past actions or from our still existing negative behaviors. Do not under-estimate the benefit of using exercise as a "safety-valve" to vent stress, anxiety or agitation. Physical activity will accomplish the following:

✓ Separate you from whatever is antagonizing you.
✓ Give you time to think, rather than act impulsively.
✓ Mop up all that extra adrenaline and cortisol that makes you feel shaky, uncomfortable and potentially irrational.

Exercise is also a coping skill that helps address one of the addict's worst enemies: isolation. As my sponsor Martha always says, "Your disease wants to kill you. But first it has to get you alone." Well, if I'm at the gym, or playing softball with my teammates, I'm certainly not at home alone, listening to my addiction tell me lies about how "we" are doing: "Don't worry, Shelley. We just need to put the right plan in place to manage it better this time. Yeah. Rules. Then we can use again and it will be okay."

How else are exercise and fitness a coping skill? Well, fitness training and competitive exercise naturally build mental strength and discipline and encourage new behaviors and new ways of thinking. They help you follow through and achieve things, which builds self-confidence, self-image and self-esteem. Setting achievable goals and targets gets us focused on the positive and helps block the kinds of thinking that lead to relapse.

Learning to Ask for Help: One of the biggest self-imposed stumbling blocks addicts and alcoholics face is that of being too (fill in the blank) proud, stubborn, self-important, scared, stupid, guilty, shame-ridden, cynical, or suspicious to ask for help. I was all of those when I was using. When I look back on my early sobriety, sometimes I wonder how I made it with my head full of all of that negativity.

I guess the first thing I learned was that I was not alone. And I also realized that I first asked for help by going to my primary care doctor. That first request for help led to folks in AA offering to help and support me – for free! Imagine that! But initially, I had to overcome my old thinking patterns and values about how asking for help made me appear weak, left me vulnerable and was embarrassing. Eventually, I became more comfortable with the concept that asking for help was a good idea, especially if I had any desire to stay clean and sober.

So how do exercise or fitness activities play into getting over our reticence to ask for help? Easy. You can't do them alone. You don't go into a basketball game saying, "Hey, I'll take on all five of you by myself." If you're going to play singles tennis, you need someone to play against. If you want to lift more weights, you might need to get someone to spot you, so you can lift beyond your total muscle fatigue point.

I know if I presented this in group, there would inevitably be the skeptic who would say, "Yeah, Shelley, but people do get sober and stay sober by themselves. And people can go running alone or hit tennis balls against the wall instead of at someone."

All true. But I also tell my clients that people win the lottery. But it hasn't been you, has it? I also ask the skeptic to tell me how "going it alone" worked out the last time.

It has not only been my own experience, but that of hundreds with whom I have spoken. They admit their relapses began when they started cutting themselves off from others, isolating, and not following through on relatively small things – like working out regularly, or walking the dog mornings, or having Sunday dinner with the folks. Or asking for help. My question to the skeptic is why are you unwilling to try something different when your way has left you with a history of relapses?

There is a saying in AA about "self-will run riot." This alludes to the selfishness and self-centeredness of the alcoholic (addict). It is these old behaviors and attitudes that must change if we are to remain abstinent and become productive, helpful and fulfilled members of society.

I would add that those who go it alone are missing the pleasure of the company of others. And they are, in all likelihood, slowing the development of their progress, skills and strengths. Humans are, by nature, social creatures. We do better with each other, and we help others to become better as we improve.

My opinion is that addictive thinking and fear of change are in part human nature and in part the brain disease of addiction. Recovery means reprogramming our brains. This reprogramming results from thinking and behaving in new ways. And from being open-minded and willing. If we are to recover, we must do things differently.

Self-Efficacy: Fitness activities promote healthy goal-setting. Regularly attaining measurable goals, no matter how small, establishes a pattern of "winning" behavior. This winning behavior flows over to other areas of our lives.

One way exercise assists in building self-efficacy (your capacity to handle problems, take care of business and generate positive results) is in allowing the individual to set achievable goals that result in "scoring a win" each day. Here is a classic example of my "Small Wins^SM" philosophy in action.

Amy was a 72 year-old alcoholic and a fall risk. After 10 days of detox, Amy still could not walk 30 feet without becoming winded, unsteady and unable to continue. On her first day at the gym all she could do was walk unsteadily (with assistance from other clients) from the van into the gym and sit down until it was time to leave.

The next day, Amy wanted to try more. I walked with Amy to steady her, to help her "take risk" and, most importantly, to ensure she did not fall. I had Amy do "sets" of walks between chairs, with a five-minute rest between each walk. I encouraged her to push herself, but not too hard. Amy walked between two chairs set 20 feet apart, resting at either end.

At the end of two weeks Amy graduated from the chair exercise to being able to walk around the indoor track (200 meters) without assistance. By four weeks, she could walk four laps and ride a stationary recumbent bike for 10 minutes. As she became steadier on her feet and more self-sufficient, her mood improved dramatically. Very importantly, she became a role model for younger, healthier clients. Effectively, Amy's efforts to overcome her age and alcohol-related degeneration served to motivate (or shame) the "slackers" into action.

At residential-treatment departure Amy was asked if "fitness group" had helped her and, if so, how? Beyond the physical improvements, which she could measure objectively, Amy described feeling happy and more confident.

"I feel like I can take care of myself again. I honestly thought I was just too old and had done too much damage to myself to be of any use. I was afraid I would end up in a nursing home. I didn't realize I could do as much as I have. I believe that I can do even more."

As importantly, the clinical team noticed that Amy had, over the intervening weeks, become more cooperative with her treatment protocol, presented with better mood, affect and attitude, and had generally evolved from a tired, grumpy old lady into a vibrant, hopeful, forward-looking grandmother.

The path to self-esteem and self-confidence comes from success. I don't know who said it, but there is a saying: "nothing succeeds like success."

Spirituality and Exercise

Spirituality has long been an important component in 12-step programs. Its purpose is to help the narcissistic addict understand that he is not the center of the universe (as we used to think and act like we were, when we were using). Even for the atheist, the concept of "something other than yourself," a "higher power" if you will, reminds us that we are not in control of everything. In other words, we are not responsible for, nor can we influence, every outcome.

This fact opens the door to begin to accept the world as it is. Letting go means eliminating racing and spinning thoughts, and catastrophizing about future events that are improbable at best. Losing the self-centered and obsessive negativity provides freedom of thought and a platform from which to grow.

Interestingly, research is also finding that spirituality is associated with mental health and well-being. Studies have indicated that spirituality is negatively correlated with abusive drinking. (12) One study of heroin users found that participants with high or increasing scores on a spirituality test had fewer uses of heroin (18).

However, people in recovery sometimes have trouble with the idea of spirituality. They may have lost faith, felt harmed by religion or simply be non-believers. But spirituality doesn't necessarily have to have anything to do with religion.

The word "spirit" comes from the Latin word "spiritus" which means "breath" or "to breathe." Depending on other derivations you choose, it can mean "spirit," "lightness of being," "air," or "wind." For those who feel uncomfortable with the concept of spirituality, perhaps my perspective might help. I was virulently anti-spirituality when I first entered into recovery. But my mind opened and I found a concept of spirituality that worked for me.

This concept of spirituality is really about something that is not physical. It is a positive, ethereal energy, not something I can grasp with any of my five senses. It is there as a guide, support and gentle director. Have you ever "known" something was going to happen? Had a feeling that you "shouldn't" take the car out that night, and found out the next day that there was a huge accident right at the time you would have been in the intersection? Many people, me included, feel they were somehow "guided" to that understanding. That the ability to sense such things emanates from being "in touch" with something larger, bigger and broader than themselves.

One form of spirituality is called "mindfulness." It's a form of meditation that has come from Buddhist philosophy. Essentially, mindfulness is the process of being very present-focused: "observing" thoughts and feelings as they come, objectively, without judgment. It's a very effective way to deal with overwhelming feelings.

Meditation is another form of spirituality. It involves more of a focused mind — but that focus is on something designed to block out all or any other intrusive thoughts — so that a "higher" awareness might be attained. When you meditate, time becomes meaningless. One is in that moment. There are no other considerations. There is no past or future, just an "expanded present."

You may already associate these kinds of experiences with such activities as yoga and tai chi. But I think spirituality is very closely connected to all types of exercise and athletic activity. What happens when we exercise? Quite often, it is a time for reflection, focus or meditation. We seem to find ourselves "somewhere else," but completely and totally rooted in the moment.

Sometimes, this connection can be quite intense or profound. We find ourselves performing with superior skill and endurance with seemingly little effort. It's as if everything becomes so clear and slow and simple: there are no worries about failure or thoughts of the future. We know what to do: in fact, it's as if we are being guided. The "work" becomes effortless.

This is known in sports as "being in the zone." That altered state where Olympic records and personal bests are attained. Where we might feel enlightenment and awe. Where Dwight Clark makes the impossible touchdown catch over and through multiple defenders in the 1982 San Francisco-Dallas NFC championship game. Or the U.S. hockey team beats the Russians in the 1980 Winter Olympics.

For anyone who has been in that zone, it feels like a mystical, or spiritual, experience. Granted, it's not an everyday experience. In fact, it can be rare. But even everyday exercise — long walks, runs, weightlifting, a game of basketball with friends — provides an opportunity for reflection, meditation and mindfulness that can calm anxiety, agitation and racing thoughts.

> I was working as residential support staff member with the adolescent girls program. Normally I took them to the gym. But this morning was a beautiful autumn day. The leaves were changing and the colors were vibrant. I took the girls to the park.
>
> I told them that "fitness group" today was simply going to consist of walking around the park. I asked the girls to think about AA literature and the concept of combining to-day's exercise with meditation. As we walked, I asked them to look at the changing colors of the leaves, to notice the birds and squirrels — to let their minds go into the world of nature.
>
> As we headed back to the van at the end of group, I asked whether they would like to do this again sometime. The overwhelming response was "Yes!" "I felt so free," one girl said. "I wasn't thinking about school or the problems with my Mom." "It's so peaceful," another girl told me. "It's such a change not to feel all the pressure." Most relevantly for this book, one girl simply admitted, "I like it out here. I didn't think about using [drugs] the whole time we were here."

In this day and age of being bombarded with media messag-es, television, internet, smartphone texts and email, we spend a tremendous amount of time directing and being directed by that next hit of electronic stimulus. Exercise can release us from these everyday stressors and allow us to make contact with a different plane of our existence.

At minimum, spirituality allows a break from the day-to-day, and promotes a bit of peace and tranquility. At best, it provides freedom from worry through a faith that things will be as they should and that, whatever happens, "I will be fine."

A last thought here. Viktor Frankel wrote in *Man's Search for Meaning* that the underlying consistency he found in his suicidal, depressed and/or addicted patients was a uniform lack of meaning in their lives.

It is my experience that exercise can help fill this void. Exercise promotes spirituality and it is through this spirituality that we are more apt to find meaning in our existence and recover our sense of humanity (our souls). Of all the things addiction robs of us, these are the two most damaging.

Summing It Up

The American Society of Addiction Medicine has established an assessment framework, used to place patients/clients in treatment, that measures the severity of an individuals' addiction according to six "dimensions" (ASAM PPC 2R). The following outlines how a program of fitness supports healing in each of those dimensions.

1. *Withdrawal Potential*

Exercise promotes/improves:
✓ Appetite.
✓ Body systems – digestion and elimination.
✓ Deep, restorative sleep.

Exercise reduces:
✓ Cravings.

2. *Biomedical*

Exercise improves:

✓ Cardiovascular healing.
✓ Skeletal strength.
✓ Posture.
✓ Oxygenation of brain, organs, extremities.
✓ Distribution of nutrients through the body.

Reduces/protects against:

✓ Hypertension (high blood pressure).
✓ Osteoporosis (brittle, weak bones).
✓ Diabetes, especially Type II.
✓ Chronic and degenerative disease – osteoarthritis, back and neck pain.
✓ Parkinson's disease and dementia.

3. *Emotional/Behavioral*

Exercise improves/supports/restores:

✓ Mood and sense of well-being by improving serotonin and endorphin levels.
✓ Thinking, memory and learning.
✓ Mindfulness and meditation.

Exercise decreases/reduces/limits:

✓ Anxiety and stress levels by increasing levels of GABA.
✓ Duration of anhedonia (the inability to experience happiness from once-pleasurable activities.)
✓ Depression by increasing levels of serotonin, endorphins.
✓ Angry and emotional outbursts.
✓ Racing thoughts, inability to focus.

4. Readiness to Change

Exercise promotes/increases:

✓ Self-confidence and self-esteem.

✓ Open-mindedness and willingness.

✓ Support of peers.

✓ Record of success ("Small Wins[SM]")

✓ Willingness to change.

✓ Trying something new or re-establishing old, positive habits.

5. Relapse Potential

Exercise promotes, provides, helps:

✓ Coping skills.

✓ Motivation and mental discipline.

✓ Social support, teamwork, belonging – "sticking with the winners."

✓ Engaging with new (healthy) friends in new activities.

Exercise decreases/mitigates:

✓ Relapse potential by restoring cognitive abilities.

✓ Impulsiveness and need for instant gratification.

✓ Isolation.

6. Social/Environmental

Improves/supports:

✓ Physical and emotional ability to return to work.

✓ Ability to support others.

✓ Willingness to act as a role model/example.

✓ Participation in family, social activities.

Regular, moderate-to-intense exercise has powerful, positive effects on the brain. However, any exercise is beneficial. It indicates how motivated an individual is to change his or her behavior, promotes feelings of self-esteem and is self-perpetuating. After a week or two, most of my clients want to do more than recommended, not less.

Research indicates that exercise can reduce the physiological and psychological symptoms that result from addictions. Studies in human and animal subjects confirm that exercise supports disease healing and management, improves mood disorders such as depression and anxiety, eases post-acute withdrawal symptoms, and promotes re-engaging productively in society.

The programmatic elements outlined in the next chapters provide a solid foundation of nutritional, strength and aerobic health concepts so that readers can tailor the principles to their individual needs.

5

Exercise with a Small "e"

Yes, You Can Do This!

I have had clients ranging from 75-year-olds with walkers, women eight-months pregnant, adults who had a fear of the gym/exercise because of childhood and adolescent teasing; morbidly obese men, women and adolescents; men who spent years in prison doing calisthenics and lifting weights; and former (or current) high school, college or pro athletes. All attained some degree of benefit to both their physical well-being and psychological outlook.

Why? Exercise with a small "e." The small e is inclusive of everyone. It enables everyone, — regardless of age, experience, fitness level or athletic ability — to stick with and benefit from a physical fitness program. Exercise with a small e is based on three key attitudes.

Comparing-In

In the introduction to this book, I talked about "comparing out" as one of the ways that addicts justify their addictions. They compare their self-destructive behavior to someone who is even worse. "You think I drink a lot! What about Joe! I only go out to bars on weekends! He goes out every night!" Comparing out is a great way to stay on the path of addiction. It's also a great way to stop working out almost as soon as you start.

When you exercise with a small e, you compare in, instead. The objective for everyone is that of personal achievement. With emphasis on the "personal." That achievement is measured against you – not someone else in your gym, and certainly not the Serena Williamses or Peyton Mannings' of the world. Similarly, you should compare in on what constitutes "sufficient," "moderate," or "vigorous" intensity exercise[3].

Tip for Success

Make sure you are medically cleared to exercise and know whether there are or should be any restrictions on your choice of activity and the intensity with which you perform.

Self-honesty

When you compare in, you do it only with regard to yourself. Your fitness program and the way your progress is measured are all about you, no one else.

---

3 These definitions are subjectively based. I don't want readers frightened away by imagery of pain and suffering. Worse than doing nothing at all would be setting unrealistic expectations for yourself, failing, and then closing your mind and quitting.

But this "you" is you today. Right now. Not you five, 10 or 20 years ago. Not the you who was younger and in better shape. Not the you who played sports in high school or college. Not the you who wasn't an addict, or whose body wasn't yet so debilitated by addiction. That "you" was younger, healthier, stronger. But that you is literally another person, and that person is gone. If you compare yourself to that you, you'll lose.

Like it or not, the only you who exists is the one you see in the mirror, right this second.

Patience

I have seen many, in their unbridled early enthusiasm for both sobriety and newfound health, over-do their initial attempts at exercise, imagining that they could quickly make up for years of neglect of their physical and nutritional needs. When you compare in, however, you set your expectations appropriately. You recognize your current needs and ability. You understand where you are, and how far you have to go. Above all, you demonstrate patience.

There are no shortcuts! As they say in AA and NA (Narcotics Anonymous) meetings: "It took you years to get to this point. Why would you think you can undo it in a few days or weeks?"

Exercise with a small e — comparing in, self honesty and patience — produces the "Small Wins^{SM}" I mentioned briefly in the previous chapter, and that we'll discuss further in this one. And Small Wins^{SM} provide rewards, which increase motivation, which leads to long-term commitment, which results in lasting success.

Don't Be Your Own Worst Enemy

Maybe the best way to help you understand how to exercise with a small e is an example of how you shouldn't.

Ryan was a 48-year old alcoholic with an extensive re-lapse history. He had suffered multiple alcohol-related hos-pitalizations including seizures and a mild heart attack. He was also highly educated, intelligent and an economic-pol-icy analyst for much of his career. Ryan was an example of a classic problem in recovery: he could understand every-thing he was taught in treatment and in AA, but he couldn't use what he'd learned to stay abstinent for more than a few months at a time. He was not "teachable" because he was not willing to take advice and follow direction.

I met Ryan when I had first informally initiated a fitness group. We had no access to a gym facility, so we walked/jogged to the local high school and did calisthenics, played catch, jogged and/or ran stadium stairs. I encouraged ev-eryone in the group to "start slow" by walking, engaging in light stretching and playing catch (football or Frisbee®). "The goal is to live to see another day," I would jokingly say. "Do enough to challenge yourself, but leave 'hungry.' I want you to want to come back again tomorrow."

Unfortunately, Ryan's ego wouldn't allow him to "go slow." He was intent upon keeping up with some of the younger and healthier men. He was out-of-shape, yet he was determined to try to run the eight-tenths of a mile to the high school track. He pushed himself too hard, too fast. It was like watching the hare in Aesop's "The Tortoise and the Hare." Except the hare here was forced to stop because his lungs were searing with pain, his legs were wobbly, his face was flushed, and his head was pounding. Ryan couldn't make it to our destination and woefully turned back just short of reaching the track.

The next day, as the group readied to head out, I noted Ryan was in his street clothes. All of his positive affect and enthusiasm prior to yesterday's session had evaporated.

"I'm too sore, Shelley. My legs are killing me and frankly, it's just too much," he said.

"What is too much? Walking?" I asked.

"All of it," he responded.

"What is 'all of it'?" I asked. "All you need to do is walk. And if you need to stop on the way to rest, you may. Our group objective is to take positive action, get some fresh air and begin laying the foundation of a new healthy habit."

"No, it's too much. I can't do it. I'm too sore. And honestly, I used to play tennis a couple hours a day, several times a week. Walking just isn't challenging enough to get me into shape. I'm going to stay in and do treatment work," he said, obviously attempting to compensate for giving up on exercise. "I'll exercise when I get home after treatment."

Ryan's story is a classic example of good intentions gone awry. He let his ego get the better of him. Ryan was comparing-in, but erroneously. He was comparing current-Ryan to 10-years-ago Ryan — who was still an alcoholic, but drank one-third as much and had yet to have blackouts, seizures and a cardiovascular event.

Ryan psyched himself out by not being honest with himself about his condition. He allowed his ego to get in the way by thinking he could make up for lost time by over-extending himself. He had no time for patience. In short, his unrealistic expectations resulted in his giving up, rather than starting out on a new path to physical and psychological health.

A More Personal Story

My best efforts to convince Ryan to pace himself fell upon deaf ears. But I shouldn't be too critical of him. I had made essentially the same mistakes years before.

Early in my own recovery, I tried my darndest to run and lift weights like I did in college and right after graduation. "Two-hour a day workouts! If you're not doing that, Shelley, you might as well sit in front of the TV! Anything less than two miles and an all-out lifting program is wussing out and not doing you any good!" I deludedly told myself.

How did that work out for me? Abject failure. I was not healthy enough, fit enough or psychologically motivated enough to handle the kinds of workouts I had done in my 20s. Even thinking I could do it was madness. It seems obvious now. So why wasn't it then? My big fat ego. Maybe I was trying to prove to myself that addiction didn't almost kill me. Or maybe I was intent upon self-sabotage.

What it took for me to get with the program was humility. I had to take a good look in the mirror. What came to mind was, "My, how the mighty have fallen!" I thought of the principle of unconditional acceptance I had learned in AA. "Hmm, maybe I am supposed to apply that not only to others, but *to me* as well." Duh!

So I started my health comeback by going all the way back to square one: 15 sit-ups with my feet pinned under the couch and 10 "girlie" pushups each morning for two weeks. That was it. Nothing more. Pretty humiliating for a former high school and college athlete with a slew of medals and trophies, and track and weightlifting records that stood many years.

I remember berating myself the first few days for being "such a loser." I think my shame came from the realization of just how badly I had hurt my health with my addiction, and how I had destroyed what used to be such an important part of my life. Having gained 40 pounds in sobriety and weighing north of 200 didn't help either.

But again, the principle of unconditional acceptance made the difference. To get started, I had to compare in — not to 1983 Shelley, but to 2002 Shelley. I let go of the guilt and shame over how a former collegiate athlete could have sunk so low. I needed to accept the world (in this case, my out-of-shape, overweight, neglected health) as it was, not as I remembered it or wished it were.

One saying I heard in meetings frequently when I was first clean and sober was "time takes time." Like many things in AA, I heard the words, but the real meaning somehow escaped me.

My first sponsor, Jill, used to remind me of this time-takes-time concept constantly. She stressed that there were no shortcuts in AA's 12-step program. You had to go through every step. It was a process, and it would take however much time was necessary.

Frankly, it irritated the heck out of me. I didn't want to hear it. I wanted to get things fixed NOW. I needed to "graduate" ASAP and make up for time lost to the ravages of addiction. She didn't understand!

For the longest time, I couldn't get what Jill was trying to teach me through my thick head. Then one day, a workout at the gym made me see the light.

I was on the rowing machine and I had set my goal at 20 minutes on level 5. I felt really good until I had 5 minutes remaining. Then I started getting tired. I looked again at the time: 4:48 remaining. Oh God. I didn't think I could do this…but I didn't want to give up, either. I just needed the time to go by faster.

2:26 remaining. I had an idea! I started to speed up and row harder. A lot harder. 1:50 remaining. Muscle burn and breathlessness forced me to slow. Out of nowhere, the thought occurred to me: How was rowing harder and faster supposed to make the time pass more quickly?

Answer: it won't.

As a counselor, I frequently see the same self-defeating drive and determination in clients. Just as we cannot take a shortcut, or rush, to do the hard work of recovery, we cannot take a shortcut, or rush, to repair our bodies. My experience has convinced me that, for most, an impatient rush to get back into shape, or over-extend oneself in a program of exercise, will result in unfavorable outcomes: excessive fatigue, injury, disenchantment and/or quitting.

Establishing An Exercise Mindset

"Keep coming back, it works if it you work it!" — AA saying

No one should be surprised that the same principle applies to fitness. But for many, the hardest part is continuing to "suit up and show up." So how do we maximize our capacity to "keep coming back" in the context of exercise?

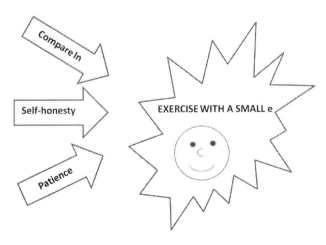

Exercise with a small e. And the three basic principles:

First, compare-in. Participation, not performance, is key. Attempt activities with which you feel comfortable, have wanted to learn and/or know you enjoy. Remember what we've learned about the limbic system. We want to stimulate it with positive emotional responses that can then become positive long-term memories. We want to reprogram ourselves with "do it again" for exercise.

Recall, the amygdala is responsible for emotional reactions and the hippocampus helps store those emotional memories long term. If we exercise/become active in ways that are appropriate to our current circumstances, abilities and conditions — and that we find fun, of interest or fulfill a pursuit or dream we have had — we are far more likely to start laying down positive emotional memories regarding physical fitness. Those memories fuel the "reward" that helps us perpetuate a new healthy habit: exercise.

Interesting Fact

Movement, especially when it involves learning new tasks (new sports or exercises you haven't done before) promotes the development of vascular endothelial growth factor and brain-derived neurotrophic factor. (2) This means that exercise promotes the growth of capillaries and blood vessels, as well as helps grow brain cells and increase brain volume.

Second, always be honest with yourself. Set a realistic schedule, with personally-appropriate fitness/activity goals.

You may be familiar with what I call *February 1 Fitness Syndrome*. This is the phenomenon in which the vast majority of people who dutifully join a gym on January 1 are no longer participating members by February 1, despite their good intentions. Why does this happen?

Because most people are not honest about who they are, what they can really do and what they can really accomplish. They commit to too many days per week, or to a 5:00 a.m. start time when they know they are not, and never have been, a morning person. Or they anticipate unrealistic results, either in terms of their ability (weight they can lift, distance they can run) or their appearance (e.g. 24 inch waist or 12 inch biceps.) Bottom line, they set goals for an image of themselves that aren't realistic.

Tell yourself the truth about your abilities, health and body type. Understand what you can do and can't do. Self-acceptance is key. You won't do yourself any favors if you over-challenge or under-challenge yourself.

Third, time takes time. Practice perseverance and patience. With exercise, recovery and life in general, results are individual and enthusiasm ebbs and flows. Perseverance gets you through the "valleys." And patience allows the full benefits of exercise to develop over time. Just like the full benefits of recovery blossom over time.

That is not to say that we won't feel immediate benefits. I've often seen people — especially those who haven't been athletic recently, or weren't very athletic to begin with — make rapid progress initially.

For the newbie, or the person who hasn't participated recently, relatively rapid progress and accelerated feelings of competence are just what the doctor ordered. They can feel very encouraged, even a bit euphoric.

It's a lot like the "pink cloud" that addicts experience in early sobriety. This refers to feeling extraordinarily happy or content, to a degree that is out of proportion to your current circumstances.

I recall my pink cloud in early recovery. It was around 30 days' sober for me. Despite family, social, financial, health and occupational ruin, and no prospects for how undo this wreckage, I felt remarkably optimistic and confident about my life and my future. How could this be? I suspect the primary reason was that I was not drinking or using. And the more days clean and sober I had under my belt, the more self-respect I had. The light I saw at the end of the tunnel was no longer the headlamp of the train about to run me down. I felt good being sober and working a program of recovery, and that overshadowed all of my other problems.

Some see the pink cloud as dangerous. The thinking here is that when it goes away, when the addict comes back down to reality, he or she can get discouraged and backslide. The same thing can happen to those who begin an exercise program, get good results at first, and then their progress slows down or even seems to stop.

But I've found that the pink cloud can be a motivating factor, as long as you realize that it doesn't last. And here is the paradox. The trick is to understand that, eventually, the pink cloud feeling is how you can feel most of the time. But this develops over time, with consistent effort.

"Over time, with consistent effort" is a fairly foreign concept to those of us programmed with the need/desire for the instant gratification our addictions provided. But exercise can help us to change those old ways of thinking and being. One of the greatest gifts exercise provides the recovering addict is teaching him to learn to live with delayed gratification.

Keep showing up. Do the work. Enjoy the "pink cloud" when it arrives. Recognize that it will wane, but will come back again in the form of peace, serenity and accomplishment. And those feelings will become more frequent and consistent over the course of your progress.

The next chapters lay out sample activities and workouts for beginner, intermediate and advanced-level participants. For those with a sport or athletic history, and some solid sobriety behind them, the beginner or intermediate levels might not be necessary. For those with little athletic background, or with disease, injury or age-related conditions, you might not advance beyond the beginner level.

Remember, the point is not to make it to the Olympics. Our purpose is to engage in activity to support our recovery from addiction, alleviate psychological conditions such as depression and anxiety, and promote long-term health and happiness.

6

Getting Started

Some of you may think you know everything you need to know and are ready to rush-headlong into the gym. For many of us, "I've got this!" was one of the first thoughts we had on the way to countless relapses. Our old ways didn't work. Here's a way that will, if you try. Actually, do more than try. So stop, take a breath, and read the exercise and nutrition suggestions that follow. Then commit to them for the next three months. You've got nothing to lose, except your old, self-defeating attitudes and behaviors....*and your addiction.*

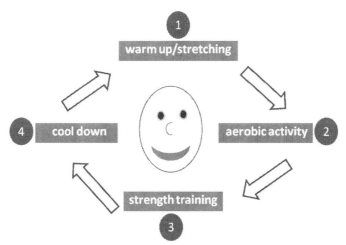

Warm-Up

The warm-up is pretty much what it sounds like. It's designed to warm up and "wake up" your body and prepare it for a more vigorous level of physical activity. A warm-up consists of slow, low-intensity movements that increase heart rate, circulation and blood flow to the muscles and extremities. (Of course, this action generates heat, hence "warm-up.") The warm up also helps promote fluid diffusion in the joints. This is analogous to using oil or WD-40 in a hinge.

Warm-up activities for intermediate or advanced clients might include brisk walking or slow jogging, light jumping jacks or other all-body movement activities. Slow walking and gentle movements would be more appropriate for those at the beginner level.

Stretching

Stretching should be a part of both the warm-up and the cool-down.

Stretching helps insure that we have good range of motion — full movement without pain or discomfort — in our muscles and joints. This keeps our bodies flexible, enabling us to use the full length and strength of our muscles.

For our purposes, we will focus on two basic types of stretching. *Static* stretching involves relatively slow movements that stop and then start again. For example, stretching your back to the point of moderate resistance, stopping and holding the position. You then ease off a bit, feel the muscles relax, and stretch again until you reach a new point of moderate resistance.

Dynamic stretching refers to continuous movements that increasingly stretch your muscles. An example would be windmilling your arms in bigger and bigger circles, steadily increasing your range of motion.

I find it easiest to do some dynamic stretches first, and complement them with static stretches. Something like jumping jacks can be used as both a warm-up and dynamic stretch. For our purposes, these are stretches you can do with some resistance, but without pain. You might find you have very little range of motion to begin with. That's okay. You might also find this doesn't feel very comfortable. Don't give up! It's important to develop more flexibility. With time it becomes easier and actually feels good.

Remember, progress not perfection. With repetition and practice, your body will gradually accommodate what you're requesting of it. Stretching increases flexibility, which promotes a full range of motion. Good flexibility reduces joint aches, pains, potential muscle tears and other injury. Flexibility and range of motion also promote maximum performance, especially in speed and agility.

You'll be pleasantly surprised when many of those nagging aches and pains dissipate. You will be better able to deal with your activities of daily living – getting in and out of the car comfortably, doing house and yard work and interacting with the kids and grandkids.

Aerobic Exercise

Aerobic activity uses oxygen to burn fat to produce energy. It is important to our purpose of supporting addiction recovery because aerobic activity has been shown scientifically to produce the positive biological and psychological results described earlier in the book.

Aerobic exercise is typically defined as activity that causes your heart rate to increase to approximately 55 percent (or higher) of maximum[4]. Aerobic activities get your heart and lungs going. They include walking, jogging, bicycling, swimming and playing basketball. Golf has varying aerobic benefit based upon whether you walk versus ride in a cart. Yoga and Pilates can have some aerobic benefit, but are actually categorized as strength and flexibility exercises.

If at all possible, start with a minimum of 10 to 12 minutes of aerobic exercise. This is how long researchers believe it takes to promote cardiovascular system improvement.(1) In addition, 10 to 12 minutes of moderate exercise trigger the production of the happy neurotransmitters discussed earlier. (3) Those at a more advanced level of fitness may require 20 to 45 minutes of activity, with maximum heart rates ranging from 55 to 90 per cent.

Don't let the numbers scare you away. Every client I have ever had felt better after any level of activity. For some, *just getting into the van* to go to the gym or the park was a big step. Forget about actually exercising. Still, upon returning to the residential facility, even those folks reported feeling better and being happier.

Why? Because they did something. Even just a little something. Even just one tiny step. And that's all it takes to feel a little better about yourself, to start improving your self-esteem, and to begin developing an attitude of "I can" instead of "I can't." So don't be afraid to start wherever you are. ANY amount of activity is fine.

This is the one instance where everyone who shows up *should* get a medal. If you're having motivation problems, think in these terms. Start where you need to start. Don't be too easy on yourself, but remember, the goal is to keep coming back. If "getting into the van and going to sit on the bleachers in the sun" is your initial goal, fine! Over time, raise your expectations. Set modest goals

---

4 The normal heart rate is 60 to 100 beats per minute. Maximum heart rate varies with age. Heart rate can be monitored the old-fashioned way, with a watch that has a second-hand. Many fitness machines have sensors to measure heart-rate and energy consumption. Inexpensive sports watches also offer calorie-counting and heart rate monitoring.

and increase them as results indicate. (Small Wins!^{SM}) Likewise, if you're feeling tired, ill or injured, dial it back.

Which Activities to Do?[5]

As you can see below, there is a large "a la cart menu" of potential aerobic activities from which to choose. Be creative. ***The best exercise is the one you want to do!*** Some of the activities in which I have engaged my clients are:

Walking: Depending upon your current physical condition, this could mean short, slow walks with a goal of completing a distance (around the block) or a time (five minutes). Brisk walking is walking as if you were late to a meeting. Brisk walking produces the best cardio results.

Jogging: The same principles apply as in walking. Don't be afraid to supplement jogging with walking. Fartlek[6] and interval training[7] methods are great ways to keep it interesting while getting in shape faster, with seemingly less effort.

Hiking: Research and choose a hike that is appropriate for your experience and fitness condition. Many parks and wilderness areas have beginner, intermediate and advanced hiking trails. A "hike" can be a walk that has hills, stairs or uneven ground in a city setting or it can be more wilderness-oriented. Keep an open mind. Be creative. Fight that PAWs tendency to think in terms of limitations or why you can't.

Cardio equipment in the gym: Treadmills, stationary bikes, ellipticals, stair climbers, spin bikes, and rowing machines are some examples of this equipment. In addition to being good for your heart, this type of exercise (except running on the treadmill) is relatively

---

5 Refer to Appendix A for a glossary of exercise/activity terms.

6 The purpose is to alternate speed and distance (or time) changes within the workout in a random fashion. An example would be eyeing a tree up ahead and sprinting to it, then slowing down and jogging to the next mailbox, then accelerating to the street corner, etc.

7 Varying of speed over set distances (or time).

easy on sore knees, backs and ankles because these machines reduce the pounding-contact we make with the ground. All (except spin bikes) have heart-rate monitors and various programs and levels of difficulty to keep you challenged mentally and physically.

Basketball: This is great for hand-eye coordination, cardio (depending upon how hard you're playing) and interactions with others. Games you can play include full or half-court teams (winner is first to 21), HORSE, Around-the-World, or just shooting around.

Catch: Frisbee®, football, baseball, tennis ball. Catch is great for hand-eye coordination, balance, increasing heart rate, and promoting teamwork.

Kickball: Team games, or kicking and catching between two people.

Tennis: Singles or doubles games, or hitting against the wall.

Football: Flag teams, 2-on-2, or running patterns.

Calisthenics: This is really more strength training, but you can add aerobic elements to it. More on this later.

Volleyball: Five or two-person team games.

Pickelball: This is kind of a cross between tennis and ping-pong. I have only seen this game on the East Coast, but it is very popular with all ages. It consists of using wooden paddles to hit a softball-sized wiffle ball back and forth over the net on a down-sized tennis court. Singles or doubles play.

Hula hoop: This is a great cardio, coordination and core[8]-strength exercise. (Why did it seem so easy to do when I was a kid?)

Swimming: This can be swimming laps or distance but can also be things like water volleyball, playing Marco Polo, or throwing a coin into the deep end and diving to retrieve it. If you can't swim, it may just be taking lessons.

---

8 Your core is basically your belly area. It consists of internal and external abdominal and oblique muscles, and the muscles supporting the spine, lower back, pelvis, and hips.

Bicycling: In this context, I mean outdoors, not on a stationary bike. Frankly, I take what I call "sissy" bike rides. I have a cruiser kind of bicycle and I go alone or get a friend(s) and we ride to sight-see and feel the wind in our hair. Of course, there are plenty who get into the spandex and "sport" of bicycling. Make it fun, however you do it. That's the key.

Ultimate Frisbee®: This is kind of like playing football, but with a Frisbee. Three to six players per team is ideal.

Frisbee® Golf: You can play this alone, but it's typically played with others. It's basically the same principle as golf, except you are attempting to make "par" or better by throwing the Frisbee® toward a pre-defined target "hole."

Golf: Ideally, walk the course. Carrying your clubs gives you the best exercise, but pulling them on a hand cart is okay. Take an electric cart only if you feel you are limited by a physical problem or lack of conditioning. If you don't want to play, you can at least get outdoors and get some benefit by going to the range and hitting a bucket of balls.

Exercise DVDs: There is so much choice available among these DVDs. And they are typically harder than what you might assume[9]. There is no reason you can't find something to suit your ability and interest.

I understand that some sports — golf for example — can require significant time and money. I am sympathetic to that, and have tried to recommend activities that can be done inexpensively and in relatively little time.

On the other hand, lack of time and money are not an excuse to avoid exercise. I have had many clients complain that they didn't

---

9 My adult and adolescent male clients generally resisted using these because they didn't consider them "exercise." There was a great deal of shock and awe when they realized they couldn't keep up with the workouts.

possess the resources to buy a couple of $10 exercise DVDs, or a $30/month gym membership, or the $5 park entrance fee to hike. These complaints are defense mechanisms 99.9 percent of the time.

Before I met them, they had the time and money to buy and use drugs. Or to sit in a bar and pay for their drinks.

So did you. Maybe you also bought three packs of cigarettes a week ($18 to $21 a week), or two monster energy drinks or Starbucks coffees each day ($5 to $12 a day).

Those things were your priorities, and you set aside the time and money for them. You were so committed, you were willing to go to just about any lengths to get them.

You have new priorities now. Your recovery. Your health. Your life. How committed to them are you? What lengths are you willing to go to get them? Get moving!

Tip for Success

Enjoy yourself. Choose a variety of exercises, activities and sports that you like, are interested in learning and can challenge you. When I engage in sports, my goals are as follows:

✓ *Don't get injured.*
✓ *Have fun.*
✓ *Win!*

If it's a non-competitive activity, then my last goal is different: challenge myself. And you can often combine that with additional goals. For example, if it's a social activity, like a hike with friends, then I can combine challenge with camaraderie. If I'm alone, exercise is often an opportunity to meditate, to think through problems, or to find inspiration.

Exercise for Non-Exercisers

Exercise is good for everyone, but not everyone likes to exercise. It's critical to find something that will motivate you or your family member or client to get off the couch. Sometimes "stealth exercise" — exercise that doesn't seem like exercise — is just what the doctor ordered.

Some of the more "stealthy" exercises are things like ping-pong, air hockey, foosball and catch. HORSE and Around-the-World aren't that challenging aerobically, but they do get a person moving, practicing hand-eye coordination and having fun. I used stealthy exercise to great advantage in motivating particularly resistant clients.

Frisbee® catch is especially helpful. It promotes movement and coordination because the disc can move unpredictably in the wind. Catching a Frisbee® challenges the brain and body, because they constantly have to react and adjust.

In fact, all of the activities suggested earlier increase cerebellum functioning through movement and hand-eye coordination. They rebuild neuronal connections and muscle memory that have atrophied and lain dormant during our addictions. Exercise and movement are critical to healing and maintaining a healthy brain and body.

Get out each day and do something...anything! Do that frequently enough and before you know it, exercise will become automatic and integral to your "staying on the beam." And staying clean and sober won't feel like such a balancing act. I guarantee that both your enthusiasm and performance will improve over time.

Strength Training

Strength training, also called "resistance training" and commonly performed as weightlifting, is a core component in a robust program of fitness. Strength training and aerobic exercise produce complementary, but not identical, benefits. That's why it is important to incorporate both into any fitness program.

Strength training is anaerobic. That means "without oxygen." Anaerobic exercise involves shorter, intense bursts of activity that burn glycogen, rather than fat, for energy. (Although they are not strength training per se, sprinting, jumping and calisthenics are also anaerobic.)

The benefits of strength training include:

✓ Building more lean muscle mass[10], which helps to burn calories.
✓ Making the muscles stronger, thereby providing better support and protection for the joints. This helps not only for vigorous athletic activities, but also for those of us with arthritis and other muscular-skeletal problems, like back pain.
✓ Strengthening bones and helping to prevent osteoporosis.
✓ Enhancing physical endurance.

The stronger our muscles become, the greater endurance we have. This translates to life improvement in our exercise regimes and in our daily living. Joey's basketball game has improved because he can run harder and faster, for more of the game. Mimi can keep up better with her granddaughters at the mall, or needs to stop to rest less frequently on those trips to Disneyland.

And, of course, we experience the same kinds of psychological benefits we get from aerobic exercise. Personally, I experience

---

10 Ladies, this does not mean you're going to look like Arnold Schwarzenegger. Whether that lean muscle results in bulking up depends not only upon genetics, but also the type of lifting (weight, repetition, sets) you do.

greater inner calm when I combine aerobic and strength training than when I do aerobic training alone. For example, after I run my resulting positive mood might be a 7. But if I follow up the run with weightlifting, it might be a 9 or a 10.

And the great thing is that these feelings tend to last longer. I also find that my sleep feels deeper and more restful, and that I'm more resistant to stressful situations.

Some of my clients report the same observation.

Dante had been in treatment for approximately three months. He would play basketball at the beginning of each fitness group, then head right to the weight room. I asked Dante why he was so dedicated to doing this.

"Basketball is great," he said. But I love how I feel when I get back to the house after weightlifting. Basketball amps me up, lifting takes me down. I was really pissed off at staff for having me change rooms and roommates…again. This is like the fourth time in 6 weeks! But after basketball and weightlifting, the feelings…like the tension or whatever…it just wasn't that strong like it used to be. Even though I felt like staff was screwing with me, I rolled with their games, rather than fighting like I used to. That's what lifting does for me, besides making me look good…"

Another example:

Kate completed treatment and I saw her at an aftercare meeting. I asked her how everything was going, and if she was still working out. She said she had joined the community gym and had been able to take advantage of the discount the facility offered for those on public assistance.

"Great! How's that going?" I asked.

"I look forward to going every day," she said. "I'm up to 20 minutes on the elliptical. And I never thought I would say this, but you were right. I do love lifting. I'm still using the machines. I don't feel ready for free weights."

"That's fine. It's important you do what you're comfortable with. Why do you like lifting so much now?" I asked.

"Once I got into the gym, I started back on the routine you gave us in treatment. I noticed that when I started lifting again, I wasn't getting road rage like I used to. Someone could cut me off in traffic, and rather than screaming at him and flipping him off, I'd just think in my head, 'What a jack-ass!' But I don't go off and I don't feel like my head is going to burst. It's like I'm just more OK with stuff happening…"

Strength training helps promote executive thinking and improves our ability to resolve conflict. It's a great tool to help fight PAWs such as emotional swings, anger outbursts and black & white thinking. Another benefit of strength training is its anti-aging effects, and not only on our bodies. Strength training is thought to enhance the brain's ability to remove waste products that lead to cognitive decline.(2) It also revs up metabolic activity and produces more lean muscle mass, helping to reduce the amount of muscle we lose as we age. We look better and our brains function more efficiently.

Types of Strength Training

The great thing about strength training is that you can do it in a variety of ways. You can use various types of equipment, or literally nothing but your own body. You can do it in a gym, at home, or even at work when you have a few extra minutes.

Body weight exercises are things like push-ups and sit-ups. You can build strength in your legs by doing squats. None of these exercises require money or a gym. You can do them virtually anywhere. For squats, you can put a chair against the wall (or back yourself up to a couch) and use it for support. You can do it as robustly or gently as your abilities allow. You can repeat it if it is too easy. If an exercise is too difficult, or you can't complete it, that's OK. For instance, I cannot do full pull-ups without assistance. So I pull up as far as I can, and that's good enough. Don't hesitate to modify individual activities to better suit your needs.

There are several types of equipment that you can use to supplement your strength-training workout, either at home or at a gym.

Stability balls are those big, bouncy, burst-proof balance balls that you see in every gym. Much of the work on the stability ball involves strengthening the core muscles. Many use these balls to do abdominal workouts, including sit-ups. But they are also excellent tools to build other muscle groups, including strength in the chest and arms. Other uses include balancing the legs on the ball and doing pushups, or lying on your side with the ball between your legs and doing a side push-up, or bridge. In addition to being available at gyms, stability balls can be purchased in sporting-goods stores or online. They are relatively inexpensive and are often sold with an accompanying DVD workout.

Resistance Bands are surgical tubing or thick rubber bands that can be attached to a door, tree, or post. They provide a strength-training workout by resisting when you try to stretch them. They are sold individually and are also sometimes included with other types of exercise products, such as Pilates DVDs.

Medicine balls are soft leather or rubber-covered balls manufactured in varying sizes and weights. The traditional way to use them is to throw them back and forth with a partner. However, individual uses include holding a medicine ball while doing sit-ups, reverse sit-ups, and cardio and/or step routine exercises.

Kettle bells are metal weights with a handle. They are used primarily in swinging motions. These exercises are more advanced, and should be approached cautiously by the beginner. Like stability balls, kettle bells are used in most gyms and are also available for purchase, often with instructional DVDs, for home use.

Machine weights are part of an apparatus with stacks of weights attached to cable and pulley systems. For the novice weightlifter, machine weights are the way to go. They are easier to use than free weights, and pose less risk of injury — because the weights cannot fall on you — while still providing good results (machine weights are also used by advanced weightlifters). Machine weights are used in every gym, but can be cost-prohibitive to purchase for personal use. However, there are some home options that might have more affordable pricing and payment terms. Note that some of these products are not comprised of stacks of weights, but use resistance technology.

Free weights are exactly that: weights that you lift entirely through your own power, with no other support. They are used to do essentially the same exercises that machine weights do, but with greater risk of injury — because the weights can fall on you — but also with greater results. In addition to simply pushing or pulling the weight, you have to keep it in balance. Your body has to fire additional stabilizing muscles to ensure that the weight doesn't wobble or waver. There is also more flexibility in types of exercise and range of motion challenges. Bottom line: free weights work and strengthen more muscles than machine weights can. But unless you're a more advanced user, you'll most likely find no practical advantage to using free versus machine weights.

> ## Tip for Success
> *Never attempt to use free weights without first getting instruction in proper technique.*
>
> *When lifting free weights, make sure you have a partner spotting you. Ask anyone in the weight room. In 35 years of lifting, only once has any stranger I asked to help me said "no." The next person I asked said "no problem."*

Anaerobic activities like strength training require a different approach than aerobic activities. Because anaerobic activities result in relatively quick depletion of muscle strength and oxygenation, we have to approach such training in sets of repetitions[11] rather than non-stop action.

You can also make strength training a quasi-cardio activity. How do you do this? Supersets[12] are a great way. Use lighter weights, do more repetitions and take less, or zero, rest between sets.

Start with exercises and activities with which you feel most comfortable and coordinated. Establish a base. From there, you can try new things and slowly put greater demands upon your body.

Cool-Down

The cool-down is the most-neglected component of exercise. Slow, non-strenuous activity such as very slow jogging or walking, easy dynamic stretching and static stretching are all ways to cool down.

---

11   For instance, I bench press 100 pounds a total of 30 times. But after every 10th time, I stop to rest for a few minutes. That's three sets of 10 repetitions.

12   Engaging in a series of sets in which the "rest" period for one muscle group is activity in an opposing or other muscle group. I superset bench press (chest) with seated row (back) exercises.

It is important to bring the body's core temperature, heart rate and breathing back toward balance, or homeostasis. Cool-down activities such as walking and stretching also help to eliminate lactic acid, a waste product of muscle exercise. This reduces or even prevents the soreness you might feel in the next 24 to 48 hours. In other words, you're already starting the healing process so you are better recovered to return to exercise tomorrow!

What we don't want is what you often see at the gym or basketball court. Hard, vigorous work followed by sitting down. That only makes it harder to catch your breath. It also increases the chances of stiffness or swelling, especially in the extremities, because the blood and fluids pool, rather than recirculate throughout the body.

If I have just completed 25 minutes on the stair climber, I do not want to walk straight out to the car to drive home. Instead, I do a cool-down that is commensurate with the exercise I have just done.

Orrin was a 20-year-old who entered treatment six days earlier to recover from crack cocaine addiction. He was cleared by the doctor to participate and took this to an extreme, just like he did with his drug use. Right away he told me he was "fine" and that he didn't need to "take it slow." He said he had a lot of athletic experience and headed right over to play in a game. I gave him the benefit of the doubt and turned attention to my other clients.

Orrin wasn't much different from Ryan in his quest to prove something to himself and others. As it turned out, I think he made it through the whole game only because there were quite a few guys who wanted to play and there was active substitution going on.

When the game ended, the guys moved on to cooling down, walking, etc. Orrin didn't join them. He was "too tired." I found him sitting on the floor under one of the baskets, face flushed bright red, breathing heavily and sweating profusely.

"Hey! Are you okay?" I asked.

Orrin could barely gasp out his words. "Yeah, yeah…just …think…I need a break."

I quickly explained to him this was precisely why I had emphasized the importance of the cool down. I got him up and started walking with him. After 100 yards, Orrin seemed to catch his breath. His face was not nearly as flushed and he was steadier on his feet.

"Wow, it doesn't make sense to me, but I definitely felt a lot better walking with you than I did sitting on the floor," he said. After that, although he never followed my cool-down instructions exactly, he never sat down right after playing either. His cool-downs consisted of walks to the water fountain, stopping, chatting with his peers, walking/wandering around to see what others were doing, and heading back to the court to shoot a few baskets. Progress, not perfection.

Orrin is an extreme example, but I included his story because it typifies our natural reaction to feeling exhausted after exercise. We stop dead in our tracks and sit down. And that actually makes things worse. You recover faster if you do a cool-down activity. It simply makes sense. Standing up straight opens your chest cavity, and makes it easier to breathe. Walking helps with circulation and in preventing the pooling of fluids in the extremities. Moving also lowers the risk of getting muscle spasms and cramps.

The workouts in this book all incorporate a warm-up, stretching, aerobic and strength training, and the cool-down. This recommendation should not be considered an a la cart menu. This should always be the way you work out, with no changes or short cuts. That is the only way to produce the best results in the long-term. Beginners should not feel overwhelmed. Simply participate to the degree to which you are able. And for those who might be more advanced, I'm trying to discourage you from taking short cuts. After all, time takes time.

Workout Basics and Goals

Maintain Hydration

Do not begin your workout if you are dehydrated. Drink small amounts of water frequently throughout your workout. If it's particularly warm or you are sweating profusely over a long period of time, supplement your water intake with a sports drink that provides electrolytes like sodium, magnesium and potassium.

Eat Before Working Out?

Too often, I see morning exercisers run out of gas part way through their workout because they didn't eat breakfast, or at least a snack. There are no excuses for not planning and eating right. Grab a piece of fruit, an energy bar or a yogurt and eat it 30 minutes to an hour prior to exercise.

This is especially important for those in early recovery, as well as those with diabetic conditions. As we will learn in more detail later, low and/or wildly fluctuating blood sugar levels lead to urges and cravings that can derail recovery.

Monitor Body Temperature

The last thing you want is heat stroke or frostbite. Dress appropriately for hot or cold weather. Be aware of factors such as high humidity, desert sun, fast-moving weather fronts and long stretches of hot asphalt (especially for city running, bicycling, etc.)

Pace Yourself

Overdoing it accomplishes nothing, other than to possibly injure yourself. It won't get you in shape. It'll get you to quit instead. Set an exercise schedule with modest, achievable goals and stick to it.

In our active addiction, no one could have accused us of following through and being dependable or reliable. Here's an easy place to start practicing the recovery skill of "doing what you say you're going to do." And it's easy, because your workout is entirely on your terms. You choose what you're going to do. And please be realistic: fight the urge to be overly ambitious.

Tip for Success

Listen to your body. If something starts to hurt, back off. If you feel extremely tired, short of breath, light headed or dizzy, STOP AND ASK FOR HELP!

Write It Down

Each day, you should note (by writing down in your calendar, on your smartphone, or in a notebook) how you felt before you went to exercise. On a scale of 1 to 10, 10 being the best, how did you feel? Ask yourself the same question after the workout.

For example, I got up this morning feeling a little stressed about work, but basically happy. I'd say I'm a 6. After I worked out, my stress seems to have evaporated, my mood is enhanced and I am proud of myself for working out. Now I say I'm a 9.

When I look back over what I have written, what do I see? For some reason (Ha! We know the reasons!) every time I work out, I end up feeling better than before I worked out. Even if I felt good before, I feel even better after. Amazing!

Keeping track of your physical progress in a diary is another way to build a positive feedback loop[13]. Some of you may have done journaling. This is a tool we use in treatment to help people cope with overwhelming feelings or with sorting through thoughts.

I know when I looked back on some of my journaling from early recovery, I was astonished at how far I had come. I could compare my thinking processes of then to now. I could also see how differently I would handle situations now, versus how I did then. When those feelings of self-doubt would enter my mind — "Gee, am I really doing better? Is recovery really working for me? Am I making positive change, or am I kidding myself?" — I could look at my notes objectively and say, "Yes, absolutely, without a doubt, this is working and here is the proof!"

There are many things you can choose to track. Here are some examples:

- ✓ How many pounds have I lost (or gained if you're trying to gain lean muscle mass)? How have my dress or pants sizes changed?
- ✓ How much less insulin do I need to use?
- ✓ How much lower is my blood pressure? Resting heart rate? Cholesterol?
- ✓ How much longer (time), faster or farther can I run now? For example, it used to take me 25 minutes to walk up the

---

13 13 What happens to my brain and my habits when I keep repeating positive action? I want to do it again. And again. Here is another example of how we can use the brain/neurotransmitters/behavioral principles we learned earlier in this book to our advantage.

hill and around the bend to the old tree. Last week it took me 23 minutes. Today I made it in 21:30.
- ✓ How much have I increased the weight and/or repetitions in my weightlifting?
- ✓ How much more challenging are the settings and programs I use now on the elliptical, stair climber, treadmill, or stationary bike?

Take literally two to three minutes to write this stuff down, daily! Believe me, you will thank me later. Having that historical record of improvement is a great motivating tool for the days your enthusiasm ebbs. Having documented where we started and where we are now is a powerful catalyst for future effort. And each record of achievement reinforces the Small Wins[SM] philosophy you need to follow.

Small Wins[SM] Every Day!

I introduced the concept of Small Wins[SM] briefly in the last chapter. The Small Wins[SM] philosophy sets the foundation for your history of achievement. With Small Wins[SM], we strive for one or more positive actions or achievements each day. We should employ this practice in our fitness program as well as in our recovery lifestyle.

The Small Wins[SM] approach uses the acronym SMART to define how goals should be set. This keyword is also used in

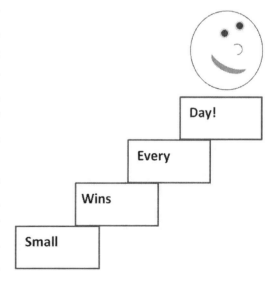

counseling and project management. SMART stands for specific, measurable, attainable, relevant and time-framed.

Specific and Measurable

In group therapy at the hospital, we have goal-setting every morning. Patients often set "read the Big Book[14]"as one of their goals for the day. Does that meet our specific and measurable criteria? Obviously not.

How about "read two sentences from the Big Book"? That's much better. If this is all you feel you can do for today, that's fine. Which of the following examples would be "specific and measurable: "I plan to walk a couple times next week" or "On Mondays, Wednesdays and Fridays, I will walk for 20 minutes?"

It's the second example, of course. With a specific and measurable goal, there is no wiggle-room. Either you walk 20 minutes each of those days, or you don't.

In the first example, how long will you walk, what days? Or will it be five minutes in the morning and five minutes in the afternoon of the last day of the week because you've procrastinated, but want to claim you achieved your "goal"? There is no real accountability involved. And it opens the door for a return to our old ways of thinking and behaviors.

Attainable

This means realistic. Is "getting an answer from the judge on my case today," an attainable goal in the context of Small Wins[SM]? No. Why? Because I cannot control what the judge might do. Furthermore, it isn't an action goal; it does not depend upon me doing something.

If I set a goal of going to the gym and walking on the tread-mill for five minutes, is that attainable? Of course it is. I either go

---

14 The Big Book is considered the basic text of Alcoholics Anonymous. It discusses the 12-step approach, how to work a program of recovery, and contains stories of those who have suffered and recovered from alcoholism. The Big Book is recommended reading for anyone suffering from alcohol or drug addiction.

or I don't. It's entirely up to me. Attainable means something you have control over: your actions. I cannot encourage you strongly enough to set Attainable goals in fitness with a capital "A." Better to under-challenge yourself and get your small win, rather than over-challenge, fall short and start sliding back into the old mind-set of "See, I knew I *couldn't* do this!"

Relevant

This relates to how the activity or objective supports our addiction recovery. In early recovery, almost anything you task yourself with, and then complete, can be relevant. Why? Because our past behaviors included making promises and commitments we never fulfilled. However, keep in mind that relevant means something that logically contributes to your goal of recovery. Going to a movie might be a task I can complete, but it doesn't contribute to your recovery like going to an AA meeting does.

I tell fitness clients that the "R" in SMART also stands for *Reasonable*. Think back to the example of Ryan. Was what he was trying to accomplish reasonable? When I thought I should be working out two hours per day in my early recovery, just like I did when I was a college athlete, was that reasonable?

Time-framed

For our purposes time-framed is always today. This is an instance where I am going to advocate feeding (to a degree) our need for instant gratification. What are we doing *today* about our recovery?

When we were using, we lacked such attributes as timeliness, reliability and dependability. All we "accomplished" was a record of failure. This became a negative feedback loop that helped to keep us in our addiction. Negative self-image and no self-worth told us we were losers who could never change, so we might as well just keep on using.

This record of failure has usually taken years to create. It's very strong. To start breaking it down, we have to chip away at it. Small Wins[SM], whether in personal behavior or in exercise, allows us immediate positive feedback. It gives us a way to start feeling better about ourselves, day by day, right away.

I know. You're thinking, "Well, what kind of half-assed goals are these and how is anyone going to get healthier or better if all they do every day is just show up at the gym or read two sentences?" Trust me. If that person has any interest in improving himself, reading two sentences will become reading 10 pages, and then a chapter. Showing up at the gym will become "Well, at least let me do the warm-up and see how I feel."

I believe that all people possess an innate sense of pride and desire to better themselves. Small Wins[SM] is a tool that lends to self-efficacy by instilling self-confidence and self-esteem. Most people do not quit things they believe they are doing well and at which they continue to see improvement. If you're getting one or more accomplishments each day, by definition you're doing well. And remember to compare-in. Measure your Small Wins[SM] against you, no one else.

Tip for Success

Always start with warm-up and stretching. A good rule of thumb here is 10 to 15 minutes. This can be walking or jogging for four to five minutes and then some light stretching. It's important that you start moving your body before you stretch. We want to get blood flowing through our muscles, and fluids to our tendons and joints. It makes it much easier to stretch if you have already generated heat through movement and enhanced circulation.

7

Taking Action

Let's start by stipulating that *no one* who is acutely intoxicated or who is suffering from acute withdrawal should be exercising. Detoxification is NOT the time to jump on the exercise bandwagon! Secondly, before starting ANY exercise or nutrition program, you should speak with your doctor and describe what it is you intend to do and whether those plans are healthy *for you and your individual circumstances.*

The activities and routines outlined in the Appendix B have something to offer for every level of ability, interest and income level. Pick what works for you. If you're a beginner, start with the goal of "suiting up and showing up" and work your way into greater challenges. If you're an intermediate, you're ready for some challenge, but start slow and work into it. For those who are advanced, try not to be overly ambitious. We're working to develop new habits and *perpetuate* them. Change activities and routines approximately every four to six weeks. Not only do we need to keep our bodies "guessing," we need to refresh our minds so that we don't associate working out with boredom or drudgery.

Reinforcing the Exercise Habit

How can we develop new, productive exercise habits?

We know that our old, drug-taking habits produced instantaneous, abundant neurotransmitter-cascade "rewards." In fact, drugs provide approximately 10 times the neurochemical reward that "normal" healthy or desirable activities do (4). This was why it was so easy to get hooked.

Those addiction-oriented pathways will be with us forever. But the less we reinforce them (by abstaining from psychoactive chemicals and addictive behaviors like gambling, excessive shopping, etc.), the more they atrophy (weaken or deteriorate). Anyone who has had to wear a cast on an arm or leg for a month or more can attest to how a lack of use results in atrophy. We want our addiction-oriented thinking and old behaviors' pathways to atrophy. One way to do that is to replace bad habits with good.

An action or activity is a habit when it is *automatic.* Learning to ride a bicycle or drive a car is automatic for most of us. We don't need to think about how we do it; we just go do it! But learning that ability required practice and repetition. Making something a habit, (like eating right), takes conscious effort and perseverance over a period of about 90 days.

Remember, these new, healthy activities, like exercise, don't have the same immediate super-strong rewards that psychoactive drugs gave us. So we must persevere even when we don't feel so good, or so rewarded. We must continue to "exercise" that new behavior on a daily basis or else it will self-extinguish.

Programming new habits is critical because we all know from experience that willpower is not enough – whether it is in recovery or maintaining an exercise or diet plan. Therefore, it is critical that we invest the time, energy and commitment to develop exercise as a habit. That means regular, consistent action augmented by Small Wins^{SM} each and every day, for at least 90 days. To prevent relapse, new healthy behaviors must become an auto-pilot function — a good habit driven by our mid-brain.

Tip for Success

Here are some goals and reminders that should always be part of your overall fitness program:

✓ *Develop aerobic capacity (more efficient delivery of blood and oxygen to the brain and muscles).*

✓ *Develop muscular strength.*

✓ *Improve endurance, power and flexibility.*

✓ *Decrease anxiety, depression and stress.*

✓ *Increase self-esteem.*

✓ *Balance workouts with aerobic and strength training.*

✓ *Engage in 20 to 30 minutes of aerobic activity for maximum benefit.*

✓ *Always work opposing muscle groups in strength training: Biceps/triceps; chest/back; quadriceps/hamstrings.*

✓ *Exercise abdominal and core areas to ease back pain and prevent back injuries.*

✓ *Use proper technique.*

✓ *Maintain regular breathing.*

✓ *Remember that more is not necessarily better.*

Understanding Where You Should Start

The workouts I've recommended (including the intermediate and advanced) are simply a generic starting place for readers[15].

---

15 There is a wealth of public, free information — including computerized charts and smart-phone applications — if you want to get more complex or detailed. The workouts contained herein, however, are there to get you going and quite sufficient to sustain just about every age and condition. Remember, these are all activities implemented with real clients in addiction treatment.

The **beginner** level is defined as being physically capable of participating in warm-up, stretching, light calisthenics, and walking and/or slow, intermittent jogging. Playing catch, shooting a basketball, and using light machine weights and cardio machines like the stationary bicycle are also appropriate.

Initially, the beginner should not exceed 50 to 60 percent of her maximum heart rate[16] during exercise. This person may never have been athletic, or has not been athletic in quite some time. Anyone over age 40, or who has a chronic medical condition, old injuries, or has recently been hospitalized or released from drug/alcohol detoxification should start as a beginner.

> ## *Tip for Success*
> *If you are new to this or haven't exercised in a long time:*
> - ✓ *Start with the minimums the first few sessions.*
> - ✓ *Feel free to add or subtract as your body, experience or endurance indicate.*
> - ✓ *Do not sacrifice proper form and range of motion to attain more reps or faster performance.*

The **intermediate** is someone who might have been athletic previously, suffered limited ill-effects from drug use or has been abstinent for a couple of months or longer. The intermediate would participate in all of the beginner exercises, as well as moderate-intensity calisthenics, strength training and other aerobic exercise. Intermediate-level participants can also play sports like flag football, basketball, tennis or hiking and climbing. Machine weights

---

16 Take the number 220 and subtract your age. Example: 220 - 53 (my age) = 167. 167 is my maximum heart rate. If my goal is to maintain 50% to 60% of max, then: 167 x .50 = 84 and 167 x .60 = 100. So I want to keep my heart rate between 84 and 100 beats per minute during my workout.

and free weights are appropriate, as are the cardio machines in the gym, with a target of 60 to 80 percent of the maximum heart rate. Duration of cardio exercise should be about 20 minutes.

The **advanced** participant has probably been clean and sober for some time: three to six months or longer. This person is already in pretty good shape, is athletically inclined and tends to be younger, rather than older. He or she can participate in all of the activities described so far, as well as intensive calisthenics and intensive aerobic activity such as running, biking, stadium-stair climbing, and super-set strength training at 70-90 percent of maximum heart rate. Cardio activity duration should range from 20 to 45 minutes.

What Will Work for You?

Beginner, intermediate and advanced sample exercise programs are listed in the Appendix B at the back of the book. Note there are two for each level: one is a workout designed to be done with a gym membership, the second is not. I want to reinforce an important concept: resources and money are not an excuse for failing to include a program of fitness in your recovery!

Neither is a lack of time. One of the biggest excuses I hear for a lack of exercise is "I don't have the time." You'll note this is the same excuse used by so many to explain their lack of 12-step meeting attendance.

All of the workouts can be completed in 40 to 70 minutes. They were designed to fit modern-day time constraints and to accommodate group schedules in residential treatment facilities. They are based on the schedule I created for the Phoenix House, where the treatment day was full and fitness group time was limited.

The time frame noted below keeps participants focused and suits the needs of all but the most advanced exercisers. Adjust the time limits to suit your needs, but note that none of these steps should be skipped.

Workout Overview

Warm-up activity	5 minutes
Static and Dynamic Stretching	5 - 10 minutes
Aerobic Activity	10 - 30 minutes
Strength Training	15 - 25 minutes
Cool down	5 - 10 minutes

The "No-Gym" workouts were designed for those who don't want or don't have a gym membership. These workouts can be done anywhere you want — indoors and out.

And for those of you with access to a gym, you have the opportunity to use the "Gym" tables. Don't forget that you can still use the "no-gym" workout, too. I suggest integrating both "gym" and "no-gym" workouts to keep body and mind challenged.

For instance, if you're a basketball player, try beginner yoga or Pilates sometime. And don't forget that there are various exercise channels or programs available on cable and satellite television that can become part of your workout. There are also DVDs and online media that you can follow, or get ideas from. As noted earlier, you can buy inexpensive packages that include DVDs and stability balls and light dumbbells. You can find stairs to climb, jogging trails, hiking or bicycling to introduce both challenge and variety. Keep it fresh and interesting!

Is that it?

Yes, good health and relapse prevention support is this simple.

What I hope to convey with these exercise templates is this: fitness is not rocket science. Anyone can do it. Fitness also does not require Herculean effort, extraordinary athleticism or talent. The only thing fitness requires is action.

As I have stated frequently, what is most important is that you choose activities you enjoy or have an interest in learning. Do them at intensity levels that suit your current abilities. You need to want to keep coming back. You will not if you over-extend yourself, or allow others to push you beyond what is comfortable, but challenging. Ninety percent of the battle is showing up. Keep Small Wins[SM] in mind!

I realize that readers are unique, with varying needs. Follow the principles of warm-up, stretching, aerobic activity, strength training and cool-down, but find what works for you and what keeps you interested. As you become more experienced, customize your workouts. Work with like-minded individuals — maybe your new sober friends! Hire a fitness trainer. Do whatever it takes to keep you engaged so you continue to reinforce the exercise habit.

As your coordination and abilities improve, add time, distance, repetitions, sets or new exercises to your routine. It all comes down to personal responsibility. Are you willing to follow this simple program and be honest with yourself?

For the Beginner

I suggest that beginner exercisers do a little of everything in their workouts for their first two to four weeks. This will develop coordination, muscle memory and the development of good form. In later weeks, if you want, you can use the outline for strength training in the intermediate and advanced groups.

Beginners are often less-than-convinced of the benefits of exercise. I wanted to share a story about a client who does not struggle with addiction, but his concerns and abilities were like those of many beginners I have seen who are in recovery.

Remo does not have a drinking or drug problem. He does, however, suffer from Parkinson's disease, which results from the dying off of dopamine neurons in the basal ganglia and nigral stratia dopamine pathway. The result is involuntary muscle tension, shaking or tremors, difficulty with balance, inflexibility, a shuffling walk and muscle weakness, among other problems.

Remo is 58 and has had Parkinson's for three years. He enjoys hiking the hills and desert around Las Vegas, but was never athletic. In fact, he told me he was teased mercilessly in school by both his peers and his P.E. teacher. He had no interest in working out in a gym, because he felt "less than" (comparing-out) and feared he would be made fun of, or get awkward looks. After repeated assurances that exercise would help his condition and that his gym fears were unfounded, he agreed to try.

Remo lacked coordination, balance and agility. I attributed that to his lack of experience in a gym and his disease. But what Remo did not lack was open-mindedness and a willingness to try.

We started with the beginner program. Everything was new to him – the cardio equipment, machine weights, free weights, incline boards (for sit-ups,) stability balls, kettle bells, etc. Our focus, however, was on the cardio equipment, simple calisthenics and the machine weights. We started with eight to ten minutes on the elliptical at level one. We also began with one set of 10 with a light weight on all weight machines.

Immediately, I could see Remo was relieved. The other gym members went about their business. No one was "watching" him. He saw other people in the gym who were struggling as much as he was, or who had severe weight problems or injuries or age-related deficiencies. And no one was laughing at them, either. If anything, the more advanced members seemed to defer to them, out of respect for their effort to overcome challenge and the odds.

As I had predicted, Remo had a huge smile on his face after our first workout. He was a bit shaky, but it was obvious to me his self-esteem increased exponentially. "I can't believe it! I feel really good! Boy, this is great stuff!" Remo beamed.

Within a month's time, Remo confided, "You know," he said, "since I've been working out, I've cut my (Parkinson's) medication back by almost 20 percent! At this rate, I'll delay by 4 months the time I forecast starting L-dopa[17]!" After two months, Remo told me that he had repeated a relatively challenging hike he had taken approximately six months earlier. "I found it much easier this time and I wasn't nearly as shaky at the end as I was before."

After three months, Remo had progressed to higher-end beginner to lower-end intermediate. He was incorporating new activities that he previously couldn't manage, such as the stair climber and leg press. He worked level two or three on the elliptical for 20 minutes and follows that with four to five minutes on the stair climber. The amount of weight he can lift has increased by approximately 30 percent. Remo has recently asked for instruction on basic training with free weights.

For the Intermediate and Advanced Exercisers

The only real difference between the beginner, intermediate and advanced workouts is the workload. The principles they follow are the same. Why is that? It's because doing the basics works! As

---

17 L-dopa is usually prescribed as the last defense medication for Parkinson's disease. L-dopa is metabolized by the body to create dopamine.

we'll see in the next chapter, whether it's nutrition or exercise, or 12-step programs, adhering to these proven, fundamental principles produces demonstrable results!

And remember, there is no rush to advance to more challenging levels of activity. It's better to err on the side of advancing too slowly, rather than too quickly. But if you're experiencing some of the following signs, it's time to "freshen up" and make adjustments to your activities.

- ✓ Your current workload has become too easy; it takes a majority of your cardio time before you hit your target heart rate.
- ✓ You're no longer feeling that burn at the end of your last set of weightlifting or calisthenics.
- ✓ It has been 4-6 weeks without a change in your program.
- ✓ You're feeling like exercise is becoming drudgery: "The same old…same old…"
- ✓ You feel "stale" or bored.
- ✓ For more advanced exercisers, you've topped out or become stuck at a certain weight or time/distance.
- ✓ You find your optimism and/or enthusiasm fading.
- ✓ You have an "itch" to want to do more!

Injury Prevention

Don't forget your warm up. Most of my "advanced" exercisers at the Phoenix House were the *worst* at warming up. They felt that they didn't really need it. Or that it was a "waste" of their precious, limited group time to lift, run and play sports.

Nothing could be further from the truth. The more strenuous the activity, the more critical the warm-up. It not only prevents injury, it promotes best-performance.

> ## *Tip for Success*
> *Strength training should alternate body parts. Traditionally I have worked out legs/lower body one day, chest and back one day, shoulders and arms one day. You do not want to do heavy lifting that focuses on the same body parts on consecutive days.*
>
> *The same with your exercise/cardio schedule. Take a break. I always advocate at least one to two days "off" per week. The body needs that time to heal, and persons in addiction recovery certainly don't need to start a new obsessively-based behavior pattern.*

Other Recommendations

One thing I always enjoy doing whenever possible is to mix up how and where I do my aerobic and strength training. Sometimes I will take a bike ride, or hike, and follow that up with a trip to the gym. Other times, I do everything in the gym. Or I'll do everything outside, doing many of the advanced no-gym strength training activities by using things I find outdoors — like stairs, benches, walls, fences, obstacles, etc.

Sometimes — due to bad weather, time restrictions or whatever — you have to exercise right where you are. The no-gym access workouts can be modified for use exercising in a restricted space — such as a hotel room, small apartment, office or even a jail cell (let's be honest, this is a very possible consequence of addiction). You can repeat the workout — do a "second set" of it, or more — if you wish.

Conclusion

It's important to keep an open mind about what constitutes "exercise." My primary objective for you is that you start, re-engage or enhance a lifestyle of movement and activity. Such a lifestyle helps prevent relapse and promotes physical and mental health. I want to break through any exercise resistance you might have and help you to understand how relatively easy it can be to support your recovery through fitness or movement activities.

You might know that in the early days of drug and alcohol rehabilitation, the treatment model was called "therapeutic community." This has some well-deserved negative connotations today. The idea then, as now, was to encourage self-efficacy by way of helping clients change behaviors, learn new skills and practice responsibility. Unfortunately, some facilities, residential staff and counselors took certain responsibilities and techniques, such as house "job functions", to extremes.

For example, clients were required to clean the floors with a toothbrush. Failures were punished through humiliation, such as having signs like "I am a thief and an addict" hung around their necks. These would be considered "human rights" violations by today's state licensing boards.

However, there was much anecdotal evidence that some of these harsh methods, such as chores from sun-up to sun-down, "worked." Why? One reason is that these clients were active physically. Activities like cleaning, cooking and gardening provided mild to moderate aerobic exercise. Lifting heavy objects (e.g. crates of apples or bags of lawn clippings) provided resistance "training."

Consider the following numbers.

Gardening activities burn between four and nine calories per minute (240-540 per hour). Washing dishes burns 155 calories per hour, mopping/vacuuming burns 252 calories per hour, and outdoor work burns between 300 and 1200 calories per hour. (5)

And some types of strenuous physical work, like chopping wood or mowing the lawn, are likely to result in 70 to 80 percent of maximum heart rate. Mopping, vacuuming, light garden work and washing the car might run at 50 to 75 percent of max.

Another reason is that exercise is an excellent distraction. It fully occupies your mind and body, making it easier to ignore the urges and cravings that can lead to relapse.

Ann's drug dealer was calling. "Oh God, what am I going to do?" she thought. She recognized the number and assumed he was nearby, probably right outside her apartment building. The problem was that Ann had just earned her 30-day AA chip. She wanted to stay clean. On the other hand…

Treatment education kicked in. Ann let the call go to voice mail. In fact, she was so scared she couldn't pick up her cell phone for fear of what her hands might do. She went to her room and picked up her landline phone. "Oh God, where was that list of phone numbers for sober support?"

She dialed the first number, but got voice mail. She hesitated, then hung up.

Next number. Dialing…#@%! Wrong number?

Third listing. Dialing….dammit. Voice mail! The selfish, blame-casting addiction voice in Ann's head kicked in. "Stupid AA program! Why isn't anyone there like they said they would be?", it whined.

She walked back into the living room. Her eyes wandered to the cell phone. "Maybe he's still downstairs or outside?" she thought. "Yes, pick up the cell and call him. Do it! Quick, before he leaves!" her addiction told her.

"No!" pleaded her voice of reason, her desire to remain free. Ann dialed the next number. Jeannie. "No way…I know she's at work… probably in a meeting…"

"Hello?" Jeannie answered!

"Oh, hey Jeannie, I'm so glad you're there. Listen, my drug dealer just called and…"

"Are you OK? I can't leave right now. Can you get yourself to a meeting?" Jeannie asked.

Ann: "Ah, no, I can't. I don't have my car and the meeting I walk to is already over."

Jeannie: "Anyone you can call to come over?"

Ann: "Ah, I barely got you on the phone. I don't know."

Jeannie: "OK, then we're just gonna chat for a while. Let's just talk this through…"

And for the next 15 minutes, Ann shared with Jeannie and Jeannie provided her experience, strength and hope. When Jeannie had to get back to work, Ann admitted she was still on edge, wound up.

Jeannie: "Hey, when was the last time you cleaned your apartment?"

Ann: "Uh, I don't know…mmm…"

Jeannie: "Here's what you're going to do. You're going to clean your apartment. Kitchen, bathroom, do the laundry, everything. You're going to stay focused on that and finish it. That should take you a couple hours. I will call you later to see how you're progressing. Got it?"

Ann: "OK."

And it worked! Ann cleaned and cleaned, and the addictive voice in her head grew quieter and quieter. Finally, it disappeared altogether. She was dumbfounded that Jeannie's seemingly silly advice had saved her butt.

Later, as Ann shared about this in a meeting, she described all that adrenaline racing through her body (her fight or flight reaction). She couldn't think straight. She just wanted to use! Of course, we know that this housework (exercise!) helped mop up her excess adrenaline and cortisol, alleviating the stress, tension and mid-brain/limbic system "thinking" that had Ann climbing the walls, ready to act impulsively. In addition, she was completely occupied, with no time or space in her mind to listen to her addiction, and give in to the urge to call her dealer.

By the way..."Ann" is really me. That's part of my story, on a sunny fall day in October, 2001.

You don't have to be anyone other than yourself. You just have to be honest with yourself. Do what you can do. Fight the "I can't" voice of self-sabotage. Your addiction wants you to quit, or give up before even trying. So don't listen when that addictive voice tells you you're being "forced" to do something you can't. Or that others will laugh at and criticize you, or that you're "no good" if you can't compete in the Iron Man next week.

When self-defeating thoughts enter your mind, replace them by asking yourself what lengths you're willing to go to for your recovery.

8

Starved by Addiction, Hooked on Food

How Addiction Starves Our Body and Brain

Because alcohol and prescription drugs are legal psychoactive substances (as is marijuana in some states), many people are lulled into thinking "it can't be that bad for me" and "it's OK because the doctor prescribed this to me." I used to be one of those people, until I found myself in the hospital, and witness to the absolute destruction alcohol (and drugs) inflict upon body and mind. "It can't/won't happen to me" devolved into "This isn't happening, ignore it," to "It's not that bad," which ended with "Oh my God, why is [insert horrible health consequences here] happening?" This chapter will help you understand why.

Brain and body damage caused by alcohol and drug use-related malnutrition affects many more people than I think we recognize.

As I noted in the introduction of this book, regular drinking (or using) often leads to abuse and dependence problems because of genetics, heredity and the principles of brain and body tolerance. Even at relatively low doses, regular use compromises our eating habits and nutritional absorption.

Part of this chapter's purpose is to demonstrate precisely why using is detrimental — no matter how often you go to yoga or how well you think you are eating. Regular use of alcohol and drugs takes a toll, not only on our brains, but on our organs and our body's ability to repair, maintain and improve itself.

Keep in mind that regular usage can trigger disease to which you're genetically predisposed. That certainly means addiction, but could also mean cancer, heart disease, diabetes and immune system disorders and other conditions.

In earlier chapters, we learned how psychoactive substances alter the way in which our brain produces, assimilates and otherwise processes neurotransmitters. Our brain tries to offset the flood of substances causing neurochemical imbalance. It increases or decreases the number of synapses; and releases or does not release enzymes, in order to try to maintain homeostasis. But these aren't the only balancing acts going on with addiction.

What is Happening to Me?

Other organs besides the brain also change in order to deal with the toxic effects of drugs, their metabolites (the chemicals the original drug breaks down into) or both.

The **liver** is the primary processing factory charged with breaking down alcohol, drugs and other toxins and getting them out of your body. The liver changes in order to deal with this extra demand. Some of these changes impact your tolerance to alcohol through alterations to enzyme and chemical reactions, and to cell structure.

While the liver is preoccupied with processing toxins, it can't effectively handle its regular duties well, such as producing and delivering glucose to the bloodstream when blood-sugar levels are low. Now you know why people with diabetes are particularly prone to ill-effects of alcohol use and why heavy drinkers without diabetes tend to get it.

Wonder why people who drink a lot tend to bruise more easily or are slower to stop bleeding? Drinking interferes with the liver's ability to produce a hormone that regulates the production of platelets: the structures that enable our blood to clot.

Of course, continuing to use alcohol moderately or heavily results in a fatty liver, alcoholic hepatitis (swelling and tenderness of the liver), jaundice (yellowing of skin and whites of eyes) and cirrhosis (scarring of the liver that leaves permanent damage). At some point, the balancing act has no effect, or causes problems of its own.

One of the most harmful effects of chronic alcohol and drug use is to alter the body's ability to absorb and process nutrients. The result is **malnutrition**. These psychoactive substances alter the body's ability to absorb and process nutrients. In many cases, the user simply doesn't eat, or is prone to eating junk foods. Here is how some drugs and alcohol result in nutritional deficits and body/mind degradation.

Alcohol damages the villi cells in the small intestine that are responsible for grabbing nutrients and delivering them to the bloodstream. Alcohol also causes changes to the stomach lining and enzymatic action in the stomach. The result: deficiencies in vitamins and minerals.

"Not true," you might say, "I always eat well, perhaps too much, especially when I'm drinking. And I take a multi-vitamin daily."

Here is the sad fact: if nutrients cannot be absorbed (or absorbed sufficiently) it doesn't matter how many vitamins you swallow! So don't kid yourself. Even if you're not to the point where your drinking replaces most or all of your meals, you're still likely to be suffering from some level of malnutrition.

There are two alcohol-related brain diseases associated with lack of B-vitamins: Wernicke's encephalopathy and Korsakoff's psychosis (wet brain or alcoholic dementia). Both are caused by a deficiency in vitamin B1 (thiamine).

Wernicke's is characterized by difficulty with vision, muscular control problems, and mental confusion. It is often reversible with proper diet including B-1. Korsakoff's psychosis is permanent and is usually preceded by Wernicke's. Korsakoff's includes memory and orientation problems, including confabulation (false stories or remembrances believed to be fact, but created unconsciously to fill gaps in memory) and dementia.

Other deficiencies seen in those who are chronic alcoholics and drug addicts include losses of magnesium, calcium, vitamin A, the B-vitamins, vitamin C, vitamin D and essential amino acids. Depending upon how long and severe the addiction, vitamin and mineral imbalances can reach toxic levels. Either too little, or in some cases, too much.

For instance, in chronic alcoholics, iron levels become abnormally high, resulting in toxicity to the liver and other organs.

Opiate drug use interferes with digestive processes, slowing them to the point where some addicts don't have a bowel movement for a week or more. Constipated people tend not to eat, nor do they have the necessary digestive activity required to process the food they do eat.

Stimulant drugs, such as cocaine and methamphetamine, result in anorexia. This is a particularly dangerous situation during drug binges (where users stay awake, don't eat and consume few fluids for up to two weeks) because of the potential for arrhythmia and heart attack resulting from the loss of, or imbalance in, electrolytes (e.g. sodium, potassium, chloride, phosphate). Water-soluble vitamins like B and C are depleted rapidly during these binges, which helps explain immune system susceptibilities, open sores and infected wounds.

Marijuana tends to stimulate the appetite, but most users gorge on junk food. I have yet to see or hear of people chowing on carrot and celery sticks when they get the munchies. Planning meals and motivation are not hallmarks of cannabis use, so pizza, snack foods and fast foods become the norm. Sedentary lifestyles punctuated with constant smoking produce lungs that are inelastic and inefficient at oxygenating the blood and organs, including the brain. Cognitive decline is associated with marijuana use, especially in younger users whose brains are not yet fully developed (under age 25).

So don't lie to yourself and compare out regarding the nutritional deficits and potential body degeneration you might be suffering because you aren't a "full-blown" alcoholic with Korsakoff's psychosis. Drugs of abuse by their very nature discourage healthy eating, or eating at all. For those who do manage to eat during their addiction, the food choices are almost always simple sugars, and fatty and salty foods. Therefore, even if you haven't stopped eating in your addiction, you're still consuming foods that support addictive pathways, and provide little of the nutrition your body needs to function properly.

Are You Feeding Your Drug/Alcohol Cravings?

Have you ever seen or heard of a recovering addict or alcoholic who has reported craving lean meats, vegetables, whole grains, nuts and seeds? I haven't. And I didn't. I craved candy and chocolate; fatty, oily, and salty foods.

Why? We know that the mid-brain area is responsible for behaviors related to survival. We understand that quieting addiction is difficult because it is wound into our survival mechanism. Well, guess where food "lives"? Of course!

The amygdala, hippocampus and striatum are tied to dopaminergic pathways that motivate us to eat, feel reward and pleasure as a result, and quiet the distress we feel when we're not eating and hungry. Sound familiar?

And, as with other substance addictions, the way these dopaminergic pathways are triggered can result in food addiction — with the accompanying cravings and "withdrawal" symptoms like anxiety, irritability, restlessness, etc. You'll recognize some of these as identical to PAWs. The difference between food and substance dependence is that the latter occurs faster and more intensely, and produces tolerance more rapidly.

Interesting Fact

In case you're wondering, the often talked-about "obesity epidemic" has not been associated with food addiction (6). Exercise can also fall into this category of behavioral addictions. We don't see more exercise "addicts" for the same reasons food addiction is not epidemic despite there being no limitations of supply or opportunity for food. Onset of action, neurotransmitter stimulation, tolerance and other factors are not comparable between, for instance, heroin or crack, and exercise and food. However, the risk remains – people can and do get addicted to food and exercise. That's why we plan rest days (no exercise or workouts) into our exercise programs (days of abstinence, if you like). With food, we can mitigate the potential for food addiction by eating the foods that are most healthy, which also happen to be the least addictive!

It bears repeating: drugs, behavioral addictions (pathological gambling, compulsive sex and shopping, for example), exercise and food work in similar ways in our brains relative to how we perceive reward and are motivated to get more.

Why Sugars and Fats Are Our "Go-To" Comfort Foods

The addictive potential in food is highly dependent upon the kind of foods we are consuming. There is evidence in laboratory-animal studies, that sugars and fats trigger the same dopamine pathways implicated in addiction formation.(6) Activity occurs along the dopamine pathway attached to the nucleus accumbens — the same pathway we know is associated with addiction. Researchers further noted large increases in a molecule (delta-FosB) known to increase drug craving in the nucleus accumbens in rats that had been fed high-fat diets(6). In other studies with rats, researchers found that "...alcohol use leads to increased consumption of fatty foods and *vice versa*." (6) (p362) (my emphasis). This action is thought to occur based upon how both substances impact triglyceride (fat used for energy) levels in the blood stream.

Cravings are exacerbated by swings in blood-sugar levels. A diet of easily and quickly digestible foods, like sugar, results in a spike in blood sugar followed by an equally dramatic drop-off. These sorts of rapid-cycling ups and downs mimic the continual need we have to feed our addiction. And for the diabetic, this kind of outcome is worse than simply increased frequency and intensity of cravings. Drops in blood sugar leave us feeling not only hungry, but fatigued, irritable, light-headed and shaky. If I didn't know better, I would think I needed another drink or drug. ***In fact, in early recovery, our brains and bodies can't differentiate between the types of cravings!***

Having My Sugar and Eating It Too?

Some might think they have the answer to deal with sugar cravings. Artificial sweeteners! Diet soda. Sugar-free candies and sweets. *Sorry to disappoint.* Artificial sweeteners trip the same dopaminergic activity that real sugars do. You might not gain weight or send your blood sugar up and down like a rollercoaster, but you're reinforcing that sweets-craving brain activity. Additionally, you start to build a tolerance, because the artificial sweeteners are much sweeter than sugars. (Aspartame and saccharin are two examples of artificial sweeteners.)

Interesting Fact

Here's a question that I had early in my recovery and many clients ask me. "Can I eat something that the label states contains 'sugar alcohol'? Is there any alcohol in that?" "Yes" and "no." The name is very confusing. Sugar alcohol is not sugar like table sugar and it's not alcohol such as that in beer, wine or hard liquor. It's a low-calorie carbohydrate sweetener (approximately two calories per gram versus four calories per gram table sugar) and is derived from natural sources like fruit, vegetables and cereals. Sugar alcohol does not contain ethanol (the alcohol in our cocktails, beers, wines and spirits).

Some sugar alcohols you may see listed on food labels include sorbitol, xylitol, mannitol, lactitol, maltitol, and isomalt. These substances are slower to digest and don't spike our blood sugar. Because they are more difficult to digest, many people who over-eat these substances (e.g. eating a whole package of sugar-free breath mints at once) will find themselves with bloating, gas and possibly diarrhea.

Getting Hooked

The food manufacturers figured this all out long ago. We crave certain foods according to their "mouth feel": the consistency of how they feel in our mouths as we eat. This is especially true of fats. Lots of research and development has gone into precisely how potato and tortilla chips and other processed foods feel as we chew and swallow them.

Manufacturers have invested heavily in exploiting why and how we feel a sense of comfort and calm after eating chocolate, ice cream and meals heavy in fats. They feel good in our mouths. And they produce increases in serotonin and endorphins.

So I'm a Lab Rat?

Researchers found that rats deprived of their sugary/fatty diets exhibited opiate-like withdrawal symptoms. And when the rats on high fat/sugar diets were administered naloxone (the same drug that is given in opiate overdoses to block the opiate from binding to receptor sites), the rats demonstrated withdrawal symptoms that included tremors, chattering teeth and listlessness (6).

Eating high fat and high sugar diets creates brain-pathway changes in the same way substance addiction does. Anyone who has dieted probably recognizes this: the more sugars and fats you eat, the more you want. Tolerance. The brain is changing. These fatty/sugary foods end up replacing all others. And "good-for-you" foods just don't taste very good any more. So you don't eat them.

However, that is exactly what you need to do. If you can stick it out for a couple of weeks, the healthy food becomes more satisfying and the fresh fruit so much sweeter. Returning our brains to homeostasis! And of course, if you're actually eating because you are hungry, versus eating from stress or unpleasant feelings, you will find that veggies, fruits, a tuna fish sandwich, an energy bar or a yogurt will satisfy your needs.

"Stick it out" is analogous to delaying gratification. This principle comes up time and again in recovery. We will not get better if we act on mid-brain impulses rather than allow our frontal cortex to run the show. That means having a plan, developing coping skills and understanding and avoiding our triggers. If we can manage our impulses for sugar/fat foods, we will eventually (as quickly as a week though more likely three to four weeks) find that new (healthy) foods satiate us. Not only that, we won't experience as many ups and downs, or as much moodiness or bingeing – assuming we are eating regularly. By introducing healthy foods and eliminating junky foods, we detox ourselves and return our brains to homeostasis. And, as a bonus, we get the amino acid, vitamin and mineral content our bodies need to think, heal and function most effectively. And over time, eating right becomes a healthy habit. Rather than an effort, it becomes automatic.

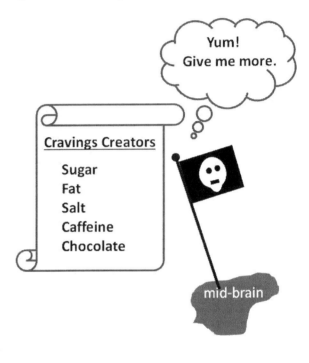

Want More Cravings?

Salt (sodium) is necessary to proper nerve, muscle and cognitive function. In our active addictions, we could have become deficient in sodium though poor nutrition, over-active kidneys, vomiting, diarrhea and excessive sweating.

However, salt also is one of those things that is associated with cravings and has been demonstrated to have an effect on brain pathways that is very similar to that of psychoactive drugs. That's because salt triggers a dopamine and opioid response. Our brains and even our taste buds develop a tolerance to salt[18], so we want more of it.

This is true for most Americans, not just those in recovery. We want salt, so food producers put it in almost everything. Check the labels on the foods you eat. You might be amazed at how much sodium is in them. As a result, even though he may have had a real need for salt initially, the recovering addict's problem can quickly become too much salt, not too little. In addition to producing un-wanted cravings, this can lead to such serious problems as high blood pressure and cardiovascular disease.

Clearly, we need salt in our diets, but the recovering person's tendency is to over-consume salt, sugars and fats. As we have seen, this promotes[19] rather than reduces urges and cravings.

Caffeine is another popular binge item for people in recovery. When we feel a bit tired or low on energy, we know that a big cup of coffee will likely remedy that situation. Isn't that good? After all, isn't fatigue a post-acute withdrawal symptom?

Where we run into trouble is over-use. Excessive caffeine only exacerbates our cravings and extends our post-acute withdrawal. That's because caffeine binds to adenosine receptor sites in the brain and body. The signal to slow down and go to sleep is blocked.

---

18 If you have ever been on a low sodium diet, or had just cut out many processed foods and all chips, pretzels and salty snacks several weeks or longer, you can attest to how darned salty those chips or French fries are when you eat them again.

19 Scientists have found that rats that were given anti (drug) craving medications lowered their intake of salt, presumably because they no longer experienced the same degree of pleasure from consuming salt. Anti-craving drugs, such as naltrexone, work by binding to the mu opioid receptors and blocking our endogenous opioid responses.

Dopamine and glutamate are not counter-balanced. We end up being more stimulated than we would naturally (7).

Immoderate caffeine use results in skipped meals, not drinking enough water, and becoming dehydrated due to caffeine's diuretic effects. Additional consequences include restlessness, irritability, insomnia and fast heartbeat or even arrhythmia. Over-use of caffeine triggers cravings via dopaminergic activity ("give me more") and suppresses appetite. This leads to low blood sugar, fatigue and depression resulting from the inevitable crash. I've also observed that heavy caffeine use is associated with heavy nicotine use. This combination is neither heart nor recovery -healthy.

My recommendation is this: if you're a coffee drinker, have one or two cups in the morning. And that's all.

And about those "energy" drinks. Take 30 seconds to think about how those products are marketed. And why you're drawn to them, like a moth to the flame. They offer short-cuts and instant gratification. And short-cuts and instant gratification are the opposite of recovery and a healthy lifestyle.

Chocolate is craved by many people, not just those in recovery. Because chocolate contains sugar, fat and caffeine, it should be obvious that this is another food that has a direct effect on our dopamine, opioid and serotonin levels. Some think our cravings for chocolate early in recovery could be associated with nutritional deficits in magnesium, calcium and phenylalanine. But if that were so, why don't we have cravings for other magnesium, calcium and phenylalanine –rich foods like milk and soy? Face it, we're craving chocolate for the fat and sugar.

Consumption of chocolate should be sparing, in my opinion. But I won't lie. I binged heavily on sweets, chocolate, diet soda, and fatty foods in my early recovery. Even with several years' recovery, I still found myself going through Hershey's mini chocolate bar, ice cream, Starburst, and potato-chip phases. My weight, mood and self-image fluctuated. If only I had I known then what I know now! For me, moderation of chocolate and sweets is just not realistic. So now these things do not go into my grocery cart. I find it much easier to abstain — with some, few, exceptions for special occasions or events.

Right-Way Eating

But the answer is not to starve yourself. That actually increases cravings and binge-eating because:

- ✓ We physically have become quite hungry.
- ✓ We feel we have "earned" a giant, gluttonous pig-out because we didn't eat breakfast or lunch.
- ✓ We are far more likely to be suffering a major drop in blood sugar, resulting in unmanageable cravings.

I recommend (and practice this myself, of course) eating five to seven smaller meals per day.

This means snack, breakfast, snack, lunch, snack, dinner and (sometimes) snack. In each of these meals, try to balance the carbohydrate, protein and fat in a 3-2-1 ratio (though that might be difficult to do with the snacks), as described in the next chapter. The carbs provide your immediate energy needs. The protein and fat are slower-burning fuel that satisfy your energy needs and satiate your hunger over the course of several hours – until your next meal or snack.

More frequent eating of smaller meals helps shrink our stomachs, so that, eventually, less food feels like more. And frequent eating is also thought to increase metabolism. While this is a healthy habit for just about everyone, it is especially beneficial for those of us who struggle with our weight and have turned to food for comfort or a substitute addiction.

Sample Menus

Because of differences in individual body chemistry and varying degrees of damage caused by your addiction it's impossible to provide detailed, individualized recommendations for specifically what you should eat and whether you might need supplements, at least in the short-run.

However, here is what I do suggest. Start by assessing your current eating habits. I recommend writing down everything you eat for the next four to seven days. Seven days is better because you'll be sure to include your weekend eating. You may be horrified by what you find.

If you're still using, or recently recovered, it's likely you'll find your current diet to be high in foods that cause cravings, and short on some, or most, of the amino acids, vitamins and minerals[20]. If you've been in recovery for some time, you still may not be eating well. Again, the best way to replenish your brain/body's needs is to eat balanced meals of complex carbohydrates, lean proteins and healthy fats.

How might you accomplish this task? I've created sample 1500 and 2000 calorie menus (see Appendix C). Keep an open mind. Avoid listening to the addictive voice say, "There is no way I can do this!" The objective is not perfect adherence. The purpose is to provide you *guidance and direction*, so that it's easier for you to figure out what works best for you! Sometimes this means trial and error. No problem. Recall, two important tenets of recovery are self-awareness and personal responsibility.

---

20 Check Appendix D for a reference on foods rich in the essential amino acids, vitamins and minerals you're most likely to be deficient in.

Recovery, and life in general, is about tacking, sailing ahead, and tacking again...

Being a Realist

If your sources of nutrition are from fast food, microwave foods, pizza or many restaurant food options, you're delaying the progress of your recovery. Trust me. I'm not being a food-Nazi. I struggle with my weight constantly. As I previously mentioned, I became obese in early recovery and, despite exercising and eating right, I still go off track from time to time and gain some unnecessary weight.

It's all about being a realist, and making the changes that take you farther from, not closer to, relapse. Nutrition plays a huge role in how quickly we regain our health and how well our recovery progresses. Foods that require more digestion, i.e., break down more slowly in the stomach, satiate our hunger and food cravings far longer.

In AA there is a acronym used: "HALT." This stands for "Hungry, Angry, Lonely, Tired" and is a question we are taught to ask ourselves when we feel urges, have cravings or are simply "off the beam." I suspect much of our anxiety, consternation and cravings can be tied directly to "Hungry" and "Tired" (sugar crash, low blood sugar). Up to 85% of mine were. I also found that the more I turned to food for comfort, the more I wanted another bag of Gummi Bears. I had learned a negative coping skill: "feel bad, eat more sugary foods." That quickly became a new behavior cycle: "eat more sugary foods, get sugar-crash, feel bad, eat more sugary foods."

If our diets are made up primarily of fatty/salty foods, sweets, caffeine and tobacco — which they *are* for so many of us in recovery — we are only exacerbating our cravings and post acute withdrawal symptoms.

9

Repair with Nutrition

Old School is the Best School

In case you haven't gotten it yet, this book is old school:

- ✓ You're not special or unique.
- ✓ You are capable of doing this.
- ✓ Stick to the basics.
- ✓ Taking action is a choice; it's *your* responsibility.
- ✓ Change will require perseverance and hard work.
- ✓ Success demands commitment and ignores excuses.

What I'm trying to strongly discourage are the tendencies we addicts and alcoholics have of trying to find the shortcut, thinking the rules apply to others, but not to us, and employing magical thinking in our dreams of a quick-fix.

As with the previous chapters, the "old school" philosophy applies to everything I have to say in this chapter about nutrition and diet. Understanding your nutrition needs and developing new eating habits are fundamental to supporting your addiction recovery. How you eat and what you eat impact your physical and psychological health. Avoiding relapse depends on your ability to eat right in order to effectively manage urges and cravings.

It's your responsibility. Hold yourself accountable.

Nutrition Basics

Remember these key facts about food and the recovery process.

- ✓ Addictions deplete the body and brain of essential nutrients.
- ✓ You can reverse this process by learning to follow a proper diet.
- ✓ Certain foods make you *more* prone to urges, cravings and possible relapse.
- ✓ Proper diet can reduce urges and cravings, decrease post-acute withdrawal and promote physiological and psychological healing.

To begin to understand how, let's start with some basic concepts. Think of the body as a refinery and food as the basic commodity from which we can produce many beneficial substances, including energy. A "calorie[21]" is a measure of that energy.

A calorie is the amount of heat required to raise the temperature of one kilogram of water, one degree Celsius. We use the calorie as a way to measure the energy value of foods. It is a tool to understand whether we are getting enough, or too much, food. If our calorie intake is more than what our bodies need for work, exercise, etc., then that extra energy can and will be stored as fat.

If we eat too few calories for our daily needs, then we start to burn fat. In more extreme situations, as we run out of fat, our bodies will burn muscle for energy. I frequently see addicts who have lost tremendous amounts of weight, including much of their muscle mass. This can be especially noticeable in men.

---

21 Calories for various foods and portions can be found on food labels, as well as on the internet and in various smart-phone applications dedicated to dietary and exercise regimes.

Food is made up of carbohydrates, protein and fat. All of them are important to our physical functioning and to our ability to stabilize mood, emotion, cravings and urges.

Carbohydrates (carbs) and protein each have four calories of energy per gram. Fat has nine calories per gram[22]. I recommend following the rule of thumb that says to consume carbohydrates, protein and fat in the following ratio: 3-2-1. Approximately 50 percent (half) of what you eat in a day should be carbohydrates. Thirty-three percent (one-third) should be protein and 17 percent (one-sixth) should be fat.

Let's look at this another way. Assume your calorie intake per day should be approximately 2000 calories. Here is how that 3-2-1 ratio breaks down:

✓ 1000 carb calories (50 percent of 2000).
✓ 660 protein calories (33 percent of 2000).
✓ 340 fat calories (17 percent of 2000).

Or, if you want to calculate in terms of grams:
✓ 250 grams of carbohydrate (1000 divided by 4).
✓ 165 grams of protein (660 divided by 4).
✓ 38 grams of fat (340 divided by 9).

This is all simple math[23]. I have found that doing it is a huge wake-up call for my clients. They find it hard to believe they are consuming as many calories as they are. Additionally, they are surprised that re-orienting their eating habits isn't as hard as they thought, and, even better, provides rapid psychological and physical benefit.

---

22 Guess how many calories alcohol has (pure alcohol, not counting the hops, barley, mixers, etc.)? Seven per gram. Seven calories devoid of any nutritional value whatsoever.

23 You can also look at food labels or do an internet search or use a smartphone app for non-labeled foods.

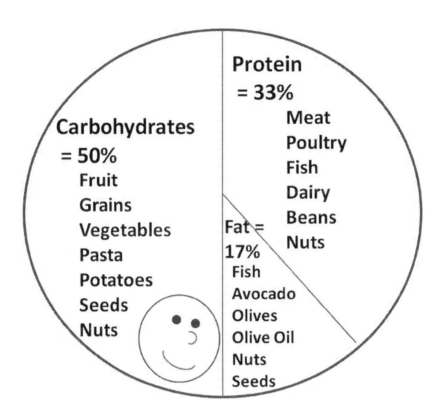

However, the last thing I want you to do is worry or get obsessive about math calculations every time you eat. What this is really about is awareness and boundaries. Being aware of what your body, brain and recovery's nutritional needs are and how to best serve them. Developing boundaries in regard to establishing limits and moderation, but not depriving yourself of occasional treats, or even excesses at Thanksgiving, birthdays or other special occasions.

Here's another theme running through this book. While I strongly advocate adhering to the basic principles I am teaching, I encourage you to personalize them. You need to creatively and flexibly apply the fundamentals to your needs, interests and abilities. Ongoing reflection, reassessment and course correction will help ensure your success. A kind of Alcoholics Anonymous Step 10^{24} for fitness and nutrition.

Here is an example of that creativity and flexibility I was talking about.

When I ran track at Stanford, the strength coaches implemented a series of weightlifting challenges, according to bodyweight, for which both men and women could compete. I wanted to weigh under 146 pounds, because I knew I could never best the throwers (who always beat the runners in weightlifting) on our team who were in the next highest weight class. I needed to lose 5 pounds, and it was a real struggle to do it. A friend introduced me to a very strict, but balanced diet, and helped me hold myself accountable. Included in this diet was a treat: a weekly trip to Haagen-Dazs for a two-scoop cup of ice cream. But I didn't get the treat if I didn't stick to the diet. So there were two incentives: a short term goal (ice cream) and a long-term goal (making weight/record-setting.) And it worked. I lost the weight, made the weight class, and set several lifting records.

Our goals in early recovery are also short and long-term in nature. Short term goals include Small Wins^{SM} in starting a new healthy lifestyle and reducing urges and cravings. You may eat too much each day and find food a comfort in early recovery. OK. That's better than using, for sure.

But we can still set an achievable goal even if we know we are over-eating, and aren't quite ready to stop. We can still eat in the 3-2-1 ratio. Maybe we replace a candy bar with an apple, or fried chicken with broiled chicken, or a McDonalds quarter-pounder

---

24 "Continued to take personal inventory, and when we were wrong, promptly admitted it." (8)

meal with the salad option, light on the dressing. We can become aware of what we're eating and how it makes us feel. And we can begin to establish boundaries via actions we can repeat on a daily basis.

Long-term goals could include setting time frames (milestones and deadlines) to significantly scale back and/or completely cut out comfort foods. Or these might be weight loss or weight-gain goals. The ultimate goal is to establish a new eating lifestyle (or re-establish one that was lost during our addictions).

Tip for Success

Generally speaking, fad diets are just not healthy. I don't care how many books are published/sold and how many people swear by some diet that required them to (for example) severely restrict carbohydrates or fast every third day. This is NOT what you should be doing to yourself—whether you're in recovery or not. There is no need to engage in extreme measures in order to maintain health, heal and support relapse prevention. There are always exceptions to the rule, but exceptions are like lottery winners – it's not you.

Fuel for the Body

Your body turns **carbohydrates** into glucose, which fuels the nervous system and produces proper nerve-cell function. Basically, your brain runs on carbs. If your diet is low on them, your body has to use protein (muscle, typically) or fat to create energy. This does not produce optimal brain function, and can affect your mood, memory and concentration (note that these symptoms are identical to some of the post-acute withdrawal symptoms discussed earlier in the book). Carbohydrates also provide energy for muscular movements/exercise.

Carbohydrates come in various forms of food we consume, including grain, cereal, bread, pasta, fruit, vegetables, nuts, seeds, sugar, cakes, donuts, cookies, and chips. But not all carbs are created equal, as I'm sure you know.

Simple carbohydrates are sugars like white or brown sugar, molasses and syrup. Some kinds — like fructose and corn syrup — are added to many of our foods in manufacturing. Others are naturally-occurring, such as the sugars present in an apple, banana or milk.

Simple carbohydrates require little digestion, so they get into our blood stream quickly. They provide fast energy. This can be very helpful if you haven't eaten and your blood sugar is low. Unfortunately, this "quick-fix" doesn't last long. This sugar high and the resulting let-down can become a cycle we should consider analogous to our substance and behavioral addictions.

Complex carbohydrates are found in vegetables, starches, nuts and seeds, and fiber. They take longer than simple carbohydrates to be digested, but the energy they provide lasts longer. We don't get the quick rush, but we also don't endure the crash, either. Some examples of complex carbohydrates are potatoes, whole grains, rice, oats, pasta, breads, lettuce, beans, peas, celery, carrots, etc. The starchier foods, like potatoes, breads and pasta, have a higher amount of carbohydrates per serving (or weight, e.g. 100 grams) than do, for example, lettuce or celery.

Your Body's Bricks and Mortar

Protein is the building block of bone, muscle, cartilage, skin and blood. It builds and repairs tissue, and creates enzymes, hormones and other body chemicals.

Foods in which proteins can be found include:

✓ Milk, cheese, cottage cheese, yogurt, eggs.
✓ Beef, lamb, pork, and game such as deer and elk.

✓ Turkey, chicken, game birds.
✓ Sunflower, pumpkin, flax, chia and other seeds.
✓ Walnuts, almonds, pistachios, chestnuts, pecans.
✓ Soy, peanuts, peas, kidney, garbanzo, pinto and navy beans.

Protein is comprised of 20 amino acids that our body uses. They are divided into two kinds. Non-essential amino acids are produced within our own bodies. **Essential amino acids** have to be acquired from food[25].

All of the amino acids are important. But this book focuses only on the essential amino acids, because the only way we can get those is by eating them. And we know that when we are under the influence, at best we are not eating well, at worst we are not eating at all. That means we risk becoming severely deficient in the essential amino acids our bodies need to function properly.

Admittedly, there are many supplements we can purchase that contain the essential amino acids our bodies need. Not only are they expensive, but for most people, they are unnecessary[26]. Because we can get them from eating well-balanced meals. Most importantly, as addicts in recovery, the first thing we usually think of to solve our problems is finding a solution in a pill or powder: a quick fix, a short-cut. And this book is all about avoiding those.

Instead, ensure that some combination of these foods are in your diet — fish, beef, chicken, turkey, pork and game, eggs and dairy products, legumes, nuts and seeds — and you'll be getting all the essential amino acids you need.

Keep in mind that cardiovascular health is best-served by eating lean meats. This simply means meat without a lot of fat in it. Choose white versus dark meat if possible when eating poultry. Lean cuts of beef and pork. And any meat can be made leaner by

---

25 See Appendix D for a chart describing the essential amino acids in more detail.
26 Vegans and vegetarians are an exception.

trimming away fat and skin. The fattier cuts (or mixes like ground beef, chicken, turkey) are typically less expensive than their leaner counterparts.

Note that certain fish (orange roughy, tuna, snapper, cod, shrimp) are excellent sources of lean protein, and may better serve the needs of some people. Fish such as salmon and trout are a healthy source of fat and protein. If you have high cholesterol, try eating egg whites rather than the entire egg. Be aware that some seafood, such as shrimp, is high in cholesterol.

It *does* cost more money to eat right. But if recovery truly is your priority, then eating right and well is also your priority. And it *can* be done on a budget, I promise you.

Fat is Not a Dirty Word

Frankly, I worry more about my clients who are too thin than those who are slightly to moderately overweight. **Fat** promotes the digestion, transport and absorption of essential vitamins and nutrients, and is a source of stored energy. Fat aids in maintaining our body temperature, healthy cell functions and (especially visceral fat) insulates body organs against shock. Fat also serves to dilute toxic chemicals before they can reach unsafe levels in the bloodstream and damage vital organs.

As with carbohydrates, some fats are better for us than others. Fish (salmon, trout, mackerel, etc.) provide the higher quality, omega-3s that are considered "heart-healthy." Seeds such as flax, sunflower and chia; avocados, olives, and nuts; and olive oil or canola oil are also a good sources of omega-3 fats.

Making Foods Work

Vitamins are chemicals that come from either plants or animals. In other words, these are organic substances. Our bodies use vitamins to promote the release of energy from carbohydrates, proteins and fats. They support tissue growth and repair, and help produce the body's healthy immune response. We also need vitamins for the maintenance and support of our reproductive and other organs. As we read in the last chapter, vitamin deficiency is a cause of temporary and permanent brain damage, especially in chronic drinkers, and affects everyone in active addiction.

Tip for Success

Fat-soluble vitamins are stored in our fat tissue and liver. The fat-soluble vitamins are A, E, D and K. Eating too much of them can be toxic, because we do not eliminate them rapidly, as we do with water-soluble vitamins (B, C). It is important to remember that you're consuming the vitamin and mineral content of whatever supplement you might be taking, PLUS that in fortified foods (like cereal, milk, protein drinks, energy bars, etc.), PLUS that naturally-occurring in meats, vegetables, grains and fruits that you eat. Read labels and be smart. More is not necessarily better.

Minerals are inorganic. That means these are substances that come from the earth. Think copper, iron, sodium, etc. Minerals are critical because of the role they play in proper nerve-impulse conduction and muscle contraction. They form the basis of many of our tissues and structures, including bones, teeth, blood and hemoglobin. Enzymatic action cannot take place without minerals. This means that many of our metabolic[27] processes — digestion,

---

27 Metabolism is the process of how the body uses food – converting it to energy or into other substances our bodies use as building blocks sustain good health and life itself. Metabolism is the process of taking something and changing it into different components that can be used as they are, combined into new substances of value, or disposed of as waste.

carrying nutrients and removing waste, properly functioning DNA and RNA — depend on our having the proper balance of minerals.

Minerals are typically discussed in terms of those that are "essential" and those that are "trace elements." We need both. However, I only describe several of the essential minerals, because we need those in greater quantities, and they are more likely to be lacking as a result of our addictive behaviors. Keep in mind that calcium, potassium and sodium are also referred to as electrolytes. Electrolytes facilitate the electrical function of our nerve cells.

I have provided further detail regarding several recovery-related vitamins and minerals in Appendix D[28].

The Human Body is Mostly Made Of…

Water. And its importance to a properly functioning body cannot be overstated. The average male body is comprised of approximately 60 percent water. The female body is approximately 55 percent water. Our blood is 70 percent water; cells are up to 80 percent water. Dehydration affects the entire body, from our brain, circulatory system and muscles, down to the individual cells.

The recommended daily intake for water is between eight and 12 cups (one cup is eight ounces). So, between 64 and 96 ounces of water per day is considered appropriate and healthy, depending on body weight. If you are exercising intensely or otherwise sweating profusely, you probably need to drink more.

---

28 The basic information you have just read is not meant to be an all-inclusive list of vitamins or minerals. Several I did not extrapolate upon include copper, selenium, phosphate, zinc, cobalt, manganese, chromium, fluoride, boron, and others. What I wanted to provide was a relatively simple foundation upon which you can better understand why it's important to try to optimize your diets, even if you aren't in recovery.

A couple of important notes for those in recovery. When we are dehydrated we become fatigued and often get a headache[29]. This frequently leads to cravings and, let's face it, as an addict/alcoholic my default is always drugs or booze to "fix" my current ailment. Even if we're not triggered to use, our "go-to" for thirst is almost always a soft-drink, coffee or juice – not water.

Unfortunately, when we attempt to rehydrate with soda, coffee, or alcohol, we consume substances that act as diuretics (causing frequent urination). We end up as dehydrated, or more so, than before. So remember: *water is the best way to rehydrate.*

As always, there's also a flip side. With all foods and activities, too much of a good thing is not better, it's bad. Even with water. And in early recovery, there's a tendency to become sort of obsessive about many things. We may find it comforting to carry, drink and refill a huge water bottle all day long. If you're in the middle of summer in Las Vegas, that might be a good idea. But too much water can dilute our minerals, especially calcium, potassium and sodium. Obviously, moderation is the key. As are individual circumstances and need.

Keep the Body in Good Working Order and the Mind Will Follow

The key to long-term abstinence is keeping the brain and body in good working order. Thus far, I've addressed our physical and nutritional needs. Is that it? Not quite. The next chapter outlines the component I believe not only helps us "put it all together," but allows us to "keep it all together."

---

29   This might be mistaken for not having eaten recently enough, but not eating regularly and being dehydrated frequently co-occur.

10

Not Your Father's Spirituality

The Great Addiction Enabler

In my experience, a disproportionate number of people with addictions avoid the concepts of spirituality or religion at all costs. If you are one of them, and are about to skip this chapter, I urge you to keep reading instead. Thoughts like

- ✓ "I don't believe in God."
- ✓ "I'm not going to let a bunch of weirdos brainwash me."
- ✓ "AA is a religious cult."
- ✓ "I'm an atheist."

have probably gotten more people to quit before they got started than any other single cause.

Shutting-Up the Addictive Voice

"Spiritual." Trust me, it might be easy for me to say now, but was not in my vocabulary back then. Not only that, but the mere mention of "spirituality" and "higher power" caused an instant flood of negative thinking to spin around inside my head.

✓ "What an idiot!"

✓ "Who is he trying to fool?"

✓ "Liar!"

✓ "Crutch."

✓ "Deluded."

✓ "Only the weak need a higher power."

✓ "Who wants to be dependent upon anything or anyone other than me?"

Ha, that last one was the epitome of irony. Why didn't I think that way when I was using?

Your Secret Weapon

Recovery is all about remaining open-minded and willing. I've stated that many times in this book.

And if you've been to treatment or to any 12-step meetings, you'll have heard it countless more times. But did you realize that being open-minded and willing are just two among many spiritual principles?

Spirituality can provide the last province of strength that walls off abstinence from relapse. Addiction and poor health are made worse by a lack of hope and meaning, and an abundance of cynicism. Spirituality (faith loosely defined) is simply the belief that something better is in store for us. It is hope.

Don't believe me? Keep reading. You'll see that "spirituality" does not mean "religious zealotry" or "cult membership."

Understanding Spirituality

From where does the concept of spirituality derive? Let's look at some definitions:

SPIRIT (from the Bing search engine dictionary)

1. life force of person: the vital force that characterizes a human being as being alive; 2. will: will or sense of self; 3. enthusiasm: enthusiasm and energy

SPIRITUAL (from dictionary.com)

1. of, pertaining to, or consisting of spirit; incorporeal.

2. of or pertaining to the spirit or soul, as distinguished from the physical nature: a spiritual approach to life.

3. closely akin in interests, attitude, outlook, etc.: "The professor's spiritual heir in linguistics."

4. of or pertaining to spirits or to spiritualists; supernatural or spiritualistic.

5. characterized by or suggesting predominance of the spirit; ethereal or delicately refined: "She is more of a spiritual type than her rowdy brother".

SPIRITUALITY

Definition of "spirituality" — Spirit comes from Latin "spiritus" which means "breath." Spirit is often thought of as what differentiates the living from the dead. "Spirituality" generally means having to do with the spirit.

Wikipedia.org describes the metaphysical concept of spirit as being different from the soul — as the spirit "develops and grows as an integral aspect of a living being."

As you can see from the above, spirituality is not necessarily defined as religious. And clearly, not everyone who has had a spiritual awakening or who considers himself spiritual ascribes to organized or any other religion. I don't.

Of course, in early recovery, this can be tough to accept. It's hard to see beyond the mountains of wreckage resulting from the actions of our past. Every previous attempt at maintaining abstinence has failed. The consequences of our addictive actions have grown exponentially. We feel like a human shipwreck, and it's difficult to imagine that something as nebulous as spirituality can possibly salvage us and help us sail again.

I also recognize that others have been raised in a religious family and that there may be scars, perhaps even trauma, related to feelings of shame, guilt, hypocrisy or disingenuousness in one's religious experience. How does one deal with that?

The answer to that is: *this* is not that. As I pointed out earlier in the book, spirituality doesn't necessarily have to do with religion in the traditional sense at all. No one is demanding that you believe something you do not, or do something you don't want to do.

Seeing the World through New Glasses

What I'm suggesting is that you simply take a new look at spirituality, through the clear set of glasses that recovery provides. There is a tremendous amount of potential upside, with no downside. My anecdotal experience – personally, with fellows in recovery, and clinically – is that finding a spiritual side to yourself, practicing spiritual principles and letting go of your need to control are keys to long-term abstinence.

What spirituality seems to do for people is this: it makes them feel *whole*. Spirituality begets *genuine* hope. And hope evolves into a faith that things will be all right. That you'll get through whatever your challenges are. That you can find the silver lining in dark clouds, rather than dwell in pessimism and fatalism. Hope lets us see *and accept* the unfolding of life as it occurs. We cease attempts to force our will upon others and to put our needs or desires above all else.

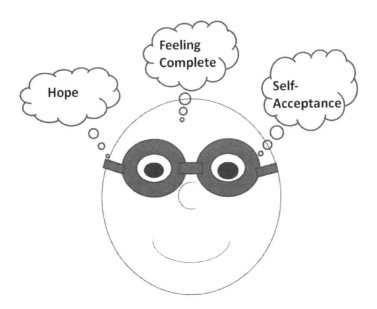

The Next Right Thing

Spirituality opens the door to our ability to find meaning and purpose in our lives. It's paradoxical that we can improve ourselves by not necessarily focusing on ourselves. This is similar to recovery's concept of "surrender." Once we admit defeat and surrender our loss to addiction, we gain power and control over our mind and body. We open our minds and allow a free flow of positive energy, good will and an uncanny ability to know (without thinking, calculation, logic or proof) where we are supposed to go and what we are supposed to do.

"Do the next right thing" is often mentioned in 12-step work. It is sometimes a conscious act, and sometimes not. I found that as my spirituality increased, my "doing the next right thing" became much more automatic and unconscious.

For those readers who are spiritual or religious I share a cautionary client experience.

Waiting for God to fix things

Denise was an Evangelical Christian who deeply believed in God and Scripture. She felt deep shame and guilt about her substance dependence and behaviors under the influence. But Denise did have an unshakeable belief in God's forgiveness and His unconditional acceptance of her as a human being.

Denise's problem was in taking action. Her belief that "more would be revealed" made her think she should wait until she received an unmistakable sign from God telling her what to do. This approach hindered many aspects of her life, including working to resolve family conflict, occupational problems and financial woes. Sadly, the result was paralysis, rather than progress.

I think that hope and faith are best applied to outcomes, not actions. It was fine for Denise to have hope and faith that her life would improve. But she still had to do something about it. She still had to act.

That meant that Denise needed to make an appointment with her boss. She needed to speak to him as an adult. She needed to explain her situation. She needed to make a case for how she would improve her punctuality and work performance. And she needed to ask if she could keep her job.

Remember the old saying, "God helps him who helps himself?"

Where did faith play a role here? In the outcome. Faith does not mean you're off the hook for action. It means you act on the things you can control and trust that the things beyond your control will resolve. From this faith, you possess the strength to weather the storms and to remain humble in the glories.

Unfortunately, we can intellectualize and learn about our condition, counseling techniques, 12-step rules and principles and still not "get it." Many I speak with talk about having had repetitive relapses until they discovered the spiritual component. "Getting" spirituality was what got their recovery engines firing on all cylinders.

Why? There is what folks in the 12-step meetings describe as the "God-shaped hole." What they mean is the incompleteness so many feel until they get out of the inside of their own heads and find something larger than themselves that transcends the five senses.

What Does "A God of My Understanding" Mean?

I recall in outpatient treatment we were asked to start "working" Step Three[30]. I cringed. Really? What sort of "higher power" or "God" would have left me days from self-destruction in the darkest recesses of self-imposed misery?

Looking back, I clearly was asking the wrong question. It should have been, "What power could possibly have saved me from myself?" I already had plenty of proof that *no persons* could stop me from destroying myself through drugs and alcohol. The awakening to get treatment had come not from someone telling me I needed to stop, but from an impossible moment of clarity in a filthy apartment, with a loaded gun on the desk, a cat on my lap and sunlight filtering through the blinds.

---

30 "Made a decision to turn our will and our lives over to the care of God, as we understood Him."(8)

But I had yet to understand that when our outpatient counselor assigned the next week's homework. Only because I was open-minded and willing to try things in a new way, I gave this task my best effort. That is not to say I didn't think it was probably a stupid waste of time, at least in my case. Indeed, I was still very different from, I egotistically thought, all these "losers" in treatment.

Nonetheless, I put forth honest effort and the best I could do *at that time*. Immediately, I started fretting about what a higher power, *my* higher power, could possibly be. Because it sure as heck wasn't some guy in a robe standing on a mountaintop. Or a tree, as one of my classmates so oddly offered.

I thought and thought and thought. It seemed so contrived, so *forced*. Eventually, I gave it a rest. "Maybe something will just come to me," I hoped. Several days later, I realized that every time I went to an AA or NA meeting, I felt a sense of peace, love and acceptance that seemed almost surreal in its ability to make me feel a part of, included, cared for and unconditionally accepted. I did not have to be the prettiest, funniest, smartest, wittiest, best athlete, wealthiest...etc. All I had to do was show up.

I had my answer! What on earth will accept me, love me and care about me, despite all of my faults and transgressions? Well? The people in meetings seemed to!

Quickly, I came to a more refined concept of God/higher power. A higher power, or God, is *not* me or you. The meetings, or better stated, the *force/energy* I felt in those meetings was not me, was not someone else and was not something I could grasp with my five senses.

Why hadn't I understood this before? My gut had told me there was more to this "spirituality stuff," but I also knew it was either beyond my comprehension at that time or, more likely, was being blocked by my prejudice that I was not going to be a hypocrite. I was not suddenly going to embrace "religion" as a way to absolve myself of what I, at the time, considered the "moral failing" of addiction. My addiction.

I'm...Still....in.......Charge

I had a need for control. I wanted to own my addiction, to believe that its beginning had been under my complete control, and that my recovery would also be under my control. That kind of thinking could be seen as admirable and responsible. But it also added immensely to the pressure I was under during my recovery. It's a common trap many in recovery step into.

What I didn't understand is that a belief in some power that is not you, that is omnipresent and is a force for good, allows for psychological relief. Understanding that many things are beyond your control, no matter how you plan or what you try to do, alleviates the struggle and fight for control of everything. After all, if we believe we have total control, don't we also then bear total responsibility? Assuming we have all the power is more infantile and egocentric than adult and realistic. It's also not remotely true.

Let me clarify. I have stated that your recovery *is* in your control. I hope it's obvious that this means *your actions* are within your control. However, some things that are not within your control are whether or when your family forgives you, what the judge rules in your case, whether you'll keep your job after showing up to work drunk or high, or what the economy or stock market are going to do in the next year. These are the kinds of things we learn to "turn over" to our higher power, or God. In other words, we learn which things to let go of and which truly are our responsibility.

Some may scoff and say this higher power stuff is just a crutch. It's not real and I'm just trying to trick people into believing something so they will feel better. Even if that were true, so what?

What will it hurt? I'm not suggesting you join the People's Temple, Heaven's Gate or David Koresh's commune. If you try it and it doesn't work, what have you lost? In fact, you have gained because you took a step out of your current comfort zone to try something new and potentially positive. By definition, that is recovery-oriented behavior.

How My Spirituality Has Evolved in Recovery

The single most significant factor influencing my worldview has been my road to near destruction and subsequent rebirth in recovery. That journey (which is ongoing) instilled in me a connection to a higher power of my own understanding and a fundamental belief that effective physical and psychological care demands more than hard-science solutions.

I am not vested in any particular path to personal or client relief, remission, cure or salvation. My approach is planned, informed and eclectic; it is not closed-minded. Individuals need to be treated individually; there are neither "standard cures" nor "right" ways of doing things. However, there are methods and principles that have proven highly successful in supporting long-term abstinence.

My spiritual worldview and evolving belief system coalesced around the time I read *Integrative Approaches to Psychology and Christianity: An Introduction to Worldview Issues, Philosophical Foundations, and Models of Integration* by David N. Entwistle (2010). I was struck by what he calls the "spy" paradigm of philosophical thought. Someone who exemplifies this way of thinking is not committed to religion. Instead, she recognizes and may co-opt a variety of theological principles and spiritual beliefs in order to advance the physical and psychological health of those whom she labors to help, including herself. The "spy" is neither fully committed to theology or to science. He uses principles from both worlds. According to Entwistle, the combination of psychology and theology can "reflect truths that are larger and more fundamental than either discipline can contain." (p.195). This succinctly described what I had philosophically believed, but had difficulty expressing.

My perspective on the supernatural is a belief in a "God" that is a force rather than a "father." Rather than demanding obedience and worship, my higher power (or God) is a positive force that is there to enhance the lives and abilities of those who seek it.

And from where might this force derive? Here is where my fascination with both the cosmos and the infinitely small comes into play. Though I can hardly claim any expertise in, or even deep comprehension of, astrophysics and particle physics, *my* concept of a higher power is based on my desire to account for the beauty, energy, precision, perfection and objectivity of the Universe.

What amazes me is that the immense forces of the Universe can be so profoundly constructive, even in the midst of being unimaginably destructive. For example, exploding stars create elements such as gold, platinum, iron, carbon, oxygen, calcium, etc. In fact, we are the products of exploding stars. Everything on this Earth, including the Earth, would simply not exist without them.

So, we can look at the exploding star as some sort of death, or we can look at it as a necessary process in building new, different and wonderful things. Rebirth. And that was the way I chose to view my own addiction and recovery. I was on the point of death, but that terrifying and destructive point led to a new, different and wonderful life.

How Can Spirituality Help My Recovery?

Addiction robs us of our very soul. It reinforces negative upon negative. Even if we were relatively optimistic people before addiction, it has long since been vanquished — replaced with repetitive failures, unfulfilled promises, lies and actions we swore we could never stoop to. We are bankrupt. Empty shells of whomever we once were. What remains is a belief we are unlovable, unreliable, immoral and worthless miscreants.

Spirituality lifts that yoke of pessimism. We learn to accept our past actions and behaviors, without condoning them or wishing to repeat them. Spirituality allows us to focus not on the exploding star, but the potential for new worlds filled with precious elements.

Some examples of recovery principles which are really spiritual principles are honesty, integrity, courage, and humility. This is hardly religious dogma, is it? Spiritual awareness affords the individual a foothold for finding tranquility in unconditional self-acceptance. Furthermore, heeding spiritual principles based on morals, ethics, service and personal responsibility promotes desirable temperamental qualities including agreeableness, openness and conscientiousness. Foundation in spiritual principles further instills courage, healthy risk-taking, honest self-awareness and the ability to change. Liberty is a huge benefit of spirituality, as we free ourselves from self-destructive, self-absorbed notions of the world and our role in it.

Recovery is an Inside Job[31]

So here is another kind of health. I have described how exercise promotes physical and psychological healing from addiction. I have done the same thing with nutrition. How does spirituality promote recovery? And what do exercise and nutrition have to do with it?

What spiritual "health" implies is that the individual assumes personal responsibility for his actions, attitudes, behaviors,

---

31 AA and NA saying.

emotions and social interplay. Furthermore, a healthy individual is responsible to others. That responsibility to others is a spiritual principle in action. Individuals who are healthy recognize themselves as imperfect beings and endeavor to engage in behaviors and thought processes that promote unconditional self-acceptance. The spiritual person is capable of fearless honesty, empathy, responsibility and service. He attempts (but doesn't always succeed) to "do the next right thing." She endeavors to give her best effort *at that moment.*

We understand from earlier in the book the role stress plays in damaging our immune system, raising cortisol levels, creating anxiety, depression, sleeplessness and potentially feelings of helplessness. None of these conditions promote recovery. In fact, they exacerbate PAWs. And stress is frequently a reason we eat poorly, eat to our feelings or are "too tired" to exercise.

One of the greatest health benefits of spirituality is in a newfound ability to handle stress. We have learned that we can only do what we can do; planning and controlling outcomes is not our job. In fact, it's impossible. This frequently automatic need to control others and outcomes is a huge source of stress in the recovering person's life.

You can see how exercise, proper nutrition and spirituality fit hand-in-glove in promoting recovery and preventing relapse. Why? They are interlocking components in our physical and psychological well-being! Exercising and eating right nurture our spiritual side. You're hardly being spiritual if you're not taking care of, or are abusing, your body!

Whether you choose to seek spirituality is one thing over which you do have control. Keep in mind that the effort and integrity you invest in spirituality yield results that no one else can grant you, or can take from you.

The Role of Forgiveness in Recovery

I want to briefly discuss another important spiritual concept: forgiveness. Many are confused by this concept, thinking that forgiving means we condone whatever wrong was done. But forgiveness is not about "letting someone off the hook."

Forgiveness is about personal freedom. Freeing our minds from a grudge or resentment or shame. Forgiveness is about making peace with someone or something. It's about letting go. If there is one thing I have found that is Kryptonite to the Superman of spirituality, it's the multitude of negative symptoms that infect us when we can't find a way to forgive. They can become like a cancer growing inside us.

So whom do we forgive? Well, the first person I would suggest forgiving is yourself. Running around with all the shame and guilt of your past behaviors and the consequences of using will not undo history. That is not to say that you didn't do bad things or behave abominably. But it's important to understand the distinction between the fact that, yes, people do bad things, but doing bad things does not necessarily mean you're a bad person.

Certainly, there are bad people — serial killer Ted Bundy is an example. But from my experience, there are relatively few truly bad people. There is a saying in the Big Book, "We don't regret the past, nor do we wish to shut the door on it." That line is a perfect metaphor for forgiveness – whether it's about forgiving yourself or forgiving another.

I am not going to propose to tell you how or when you "should" be ready to forgive. That can only come from you. But what I can do is help you better understand how not being able to forgive can impact your thought processes, actions and behaviors – and potential for relapse.

Being unable to forgive feeds our addictive nature. Why would we get clean and sober (or stop our behavioral addictions) only to throw away what we have learned about giving up the need for control? If I'm dwelling in resentment, self-hatred, grudges, obsession, fantasies of retaliation and passive-aggressive behavior, I am spending much of my brain-power and emotion on things that *cannot* be changed! And what am I not working on? Right. My recovery. And slowly repairing the wreckage of my using.

Bottom line: finding your way to forgiveness combats the build-up of negative, destructive feelings that can harm or totally derail your journey away from addiction.

It's a Process, Not an Event

It's not easy and I don't mean to imply that. This is especially the case when we are in early recovery with all of our PAWs and feeling overwhelmed by so much of what we need to do to get better. My point here is to make you aware of the importance of forgiveness to our spiritual condition.

Forgiveness is a process; it's not like snapping your fingers and all is well. It, like everything else about recovery, takes hard work. But placed into practice, your life will become fuller. You will feel freedom, serenity and peace. And most importantly, forgiveness is another thing that moves you farther from, not closer to, relapse.

I always thought my sponsor was crazy when I would tell her about some horrible person who did a bad thing to me and her response was, "pray for him" or "pray for her."

Praying for that person? I didn't even pray. I didn't know anything about that! "Just try it," she said. "There's no right or wrong way."

So I did. I would think about how that person had really hurt me. How what they'd done was unfair and wrong. But maybe their issues were bigger than mine? Maybe they were suffering in a way I didn't know about.

In no way did I let them off the hook for what they had done. But what I decided to do was to let it go. Having my head swirling with constant negativity was not "winning" or "showing them" anything.

Was I really wasting inordinate amounts of time trying to rewrite history by dwelling on people and things that had hurt me? So that I would know how to get even if they happened again?

What? Really? I want this to happen again so I can exact preemptive revenge? That's crazy. The act of "praying" and forgiving pulled me from the swamp of darkness. I started to see the light.

Rather than complaining, feeling sorry for myself and staying stuck in the past, I could get refocused on *my* recovery and how *I* was going to change.

Life *is* Like a Box of Chocolates

Life in recovery might not play out in the ways in which you might assume, demand, fantasize about, or wish for. But you have a choice over how you will react to what happens in life.

In my experiences, negativity begets pessimism, hopelessness, self-pity and relapse. Positive thinking and optimism, even in the worst of circumstances, evoke hope, faith and self-efficacy. Indeed, spirituality is that gateway to an optimistic way to search for meaning. It is also a key to peace and serenity.

For me, that came from a "spiritual awakening". What is a spiritual awakening? I think for many, me included, it means we cast away the narcissistic and self-centered thinking and behaviors that epitomized our lives during addiction. We became open-minded and humble. And please don't confuse humility with humiliation. Humiliation involves disgrace, degradation and dishonor. Humility conveys modesty, and a lack of arrogance and self-importance. AA talks about "becoming 'right-sized'." Spirituality grows as our ego deflates. We cease feeling isolated and lonely. And we begin to find more emotional balance.

The Fit between Spirituality and Sport

In this book, I have stressed the importance of exercise, good nutrition and spirituality in a successful program of recovery. Although I have, for the most part, talked about them separately, in reality they all work together.

Spiritually is a natural fit with many individually-oriented exercise activities. Walking, hiking, running, swimming, yoga, Pilates, golf and weightlifting are quite conducive to such practices as mindfulness, meditation and prayer.

Personally, I find that I spend some of my most productive time during cardio-endurance exercise. Many of the ideas for this book, and for educational presentations for clients, have come to me while on the elliptical or stair climber at the gym. Other times, I use that exercise period to channel serenity, peace and positive thinking. I admit I can be easily distracted, and having to concentrate part of my brain on the exercise leaves the rest of it free to focus on spirituality, problem-solving, reinvigorating my faith, or renewing my "gratitude list."

The same goes for eating well. How healthy and spiritual can one feel over-indulging in fatty, sugary, salty diets while TV-bingeing on the latest Law & Order marathon? As the saying goes, "Treat your body like a temple."

Consider exercise, diet, and spirituality as a three-legged stool. With all three legs, our recovery sits on that stool safely. If we remove any of the legs, the stool becomes unstable.

You see where I'm going with this. The most dependable way to prevent relapse, recover successfully and live a life of peace and serenity is to keep all three legs on the stool.

It is my hope that you will take the principles outlined in this book and begin to use them regularly. I think that, practiced enthusiastically, they will take you farther and faster in your recovery than you could possibly have imagined.

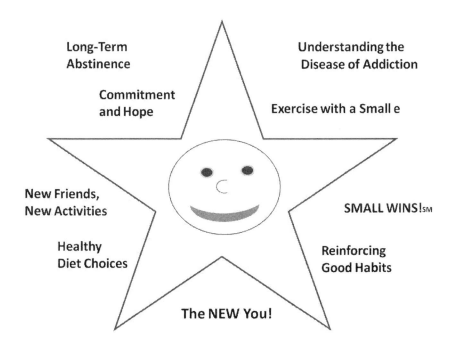

11

Afterword

The purpose of this book was to convey two things:

✓ You need to do this.
✓ You can do this!

Recovery, staying abstinent, is not easy. As I've said before, the trick isn't stopping drug/alcohol use or process addictions. The trick is *staying stopped*. Applying the principles in this book to your recovery lifestyle increases the odds of your staying stopped. Why?

✓ Exercise and proper nutrition rebalance the state of your addicted brain's neurotransmitters. You start to feel better, faster.
✓ Exercise helps you grow new neurons and increase the strength and quality of communication between brain cells. You start to think better, faster.
✓ Exercise and proper nutrition help you to minimize and overcome post-acute withdrawal symptoms faster.
✓ Proper nutrition reduces urges and cravings to use.

✓ Exercise and proper nutrition help prevent certain mental health conditions.

✓ Exercise is a great way to cope with, and prevent, urges and cravings.

✓ Exercise and proper nutrition play a key role in the management of diseases and aging-related deficiencies or problems.

✓ Exercise provides an escape from isolationism and opens the door to engaging with healthy people, places and things.

✓ Exercise and proper nutrition are great self-esteem and self-confidence builders.

✓ Exercise helps with your ability to solve conflicts and reduce stress.

✓ A regular program of exercise and healthy eating is associated with more frequent feelings of well-being, calm and serenity.

That's why you need to do this. But can you do this?

Absolutely! I am astounded at how many of my clients who are initially resistant to exercise quickly become my biggest "fitness group" proponents. I simply ask, "What's wrong? Are you afraid you might feel better and actually want to stay abstinent?"

Those old patterns of self-sabotage try very hard to keep you "stuck" and make you fail. Remember how we used to think of addiction as our "best friend"? Recall how quickly it became our only "friend"? And the entire time, we were willfully ignorant that addiction was never our friend, only our mortal enemy.

Don't give in to it. Listen to your heart, not your addiction. Make exercise and a healthy diet your new best friends. True friends. Friends who have no interest in killing you. Or in stealing your soul.

These new friends form the bedrock foundation of your abstinence. From there, you are free to build a skyscraper of recovery as tall as you are willing.

Good luck, my friends. Stay strong.

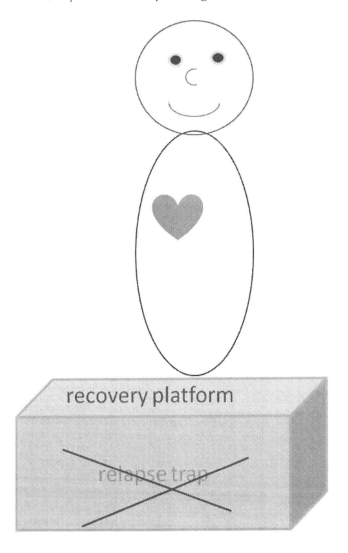

recovery platform

relapse trap

APPENDIX A

Exercise Glossary

General Terms

Following are definitions, terms and simple calculations that form the basis of any exercise program.

Aerobic: Any activity that uses oxygen in the production of energy. These are generally activities that are of longer duration. Examples include walking, jogging, playing sports, and bicycling.

Anaerobic: Activities that don't use oxygen in the production of energy. These are generally activities demanding short, intense bursts of movement. Examples include lifting weight, 40-yard sprints and swinging a baseball bat.

Antagonist Muscles: Muscles that flex. Think of your bicep. This flexes your arm toward you.

Agonist Muscles: Muscles that extend. Think of your triceps. This extends your arm away from you.

Calisthenics: Physical exercises using your own body weight, such as push-ups, sit-ups, jumping jacks, windmills, shadow-boxing, jumping onto a platform or bench.

Cardio or Cardiovascular Exercise: In this book the term is used as a synonym for aerobic exercise. Cardio exercise requires oxygen and makes longer-duration demands of the heart and lungs than does short-burst, anaerobic exercise. Examples include jogging, walking, swimming and dance.

Cool Down: Gentle activities such as walking and light stretching that promote the body's return to homeostasis: lowered respiration, heart rate and body temperature. This also promotes removal of lactic acid/waste byproducts resulting from exercise.

Core: People often think this is the same as abdominal work. Core work includes the abdominals but is more comprehensive. The core area consists of internal and external abdominal and oblique (the muscles at the sides of your "six-pack") muscles, and the muscles that support the spine, lower back, pelvis, and hips.

Endurance: The ability to become less fatigued by exercise and to go farther or perform over longer periods of time. "Over three months, John developed the endurance to be able to run four miles."

Flexibility: The degree to which you have full range of motion in your joints. Gymnasts and yoga practitioners tend to have tremendous flexibility.

Maximum Heart Rate: The fastest you heart should beat, given your age, during exercise. The simplest way to calculate it (there are others) is to subtract your age from 220. Example: 220 - 53 (my age) = 167. When I work out on the elliptical, I try to maintain an average heart rate of approximately 75 to 85% of max. This would be between 125 (167 x .75) and 142 (167 x .85) beats per minute.

MET: Metabolic Equivalent. You will see this measure on most cardio equipment in the gym. One MET is the equivalent of your oxygen and caloric needs at rest. If the stair climber I am using indicates I am working at seven METs, that means the work I am doing is requiring seven times the oxygen and calories I use at rest.

Range of Motion: The degree to which you can move the joints of your body: your shoulders, hips, knees, etc. Full range of motion insures flexibility. Some people, gymnasts and yoga practitioners for example, tend to have tremendous range of motion and flexibility. On the other hand, many of us have less-than-complete range of motion in at least some parts of our bodies. Our objective in stretching is to increase our range of motion and flexibility. Range of motion also applies in other activities, such as weight lifting. A full range of motion for a bench press would be to bring the bar all the way down to our chest, then push it up to the fullest extent just short of locking out our elbows.

Resistance Training: The terms "resistance" and "strength" training are used interchangeably. Resistance/strength activities include weight lifting, use of body weight for resistance, and other implements such as elastic bands, kettle bells, stability balls and medicine balls. The purpose is in challenging muscles in isometric (muscle contraction without movement, like a plank pose), isotonic (constant resistance, like lifting a weight) and isokinetic (variable resistance like that with an elastic band) ways to develop muscle mass and strength.

Strength Training: See resistance training.

Stretching: The measured pulling or stretching of muscles, usually done during a warm up to help loosen muscles and joints.

Static Stretching: This is the stretch-and-hold technique. An example would be bending over, touching one's toes, and holding that position without bouncing or otherwise moving.

Dynamic Stretching: This is stretching via controlled movement. An example is moving one's arms in bigger and bigger circles to increase the stretch.

Watt: A watt is a measure of power. It describes how much energy is being expended. Many types of cardio equipment track your watts. It's a way to compare how much effort you put into identical workout routines — such as setting the stair climber for 10 minutes on level 5 and comparing the watts expended today to those yesterday.

Warm Up: Designed to warm up and "wake up" your body and prepare it for a more vigorous level of physical activity. A warm up consists of slow, low-intensity movements that increase heart rate, circulation and blood flow to the muscles and extremities. (Of course, this action generates heat, hence "warm-up.") The warm up also helps promote fluid diffusion in the joints.

Caloric Terms

Base Metabolic Rate: A calculation that determines how many calories a person uses when at rest, i.e. sleeping or watching television. This number is individual and is affected by sex, age, weight and hereditary factors. There are numerous calculators available online that give a close estimate. Knowing this number helps to determine how much food (caloric increase) and exercise (caloric decrease) one might need in meeting weight loss or gain goals.

Calorie: (kcal) A calorie is a the amount of heat or energy it takes to raise one kilogram of water one degree Celsius at one atmosphere (sea level). This is the amount of energy our bodies need to burn one calorie of the food we eat. This is significant because if we are not active enough or do not exercise enough to produce that energy, the excess calories we eat are stored as fat.

Calories per Pound of Fat: Approximately 3500 calories equal one pound of fat. Therefore, to lose one pound per week one must either cut 3500 calories out of his diet, or exercise and diet (recommended) to net a reduction of 3500 calories.

Calories per Gram:
- ✓ Four calories per gram of carbohydrate.
- ✓ Four calories per gram of protein.
- ✓ Nine calories per gram of fat.
- ✓ Seven empty (non-nutritional) calories per gram of alcohol.

Metabolism: In regard to exercise, the rate at which the body converts fuel to energy. In regard to drug and alcohol intake, the rate at which the body breaks down any given substance into metabolites (smaller, different molecules) and eliminates them from the body.

Exercise/Activity Terms

Circuit Training: Frequently thought of in the context of machine weights, but essentially means any exercise activities done in a rotation. For example, doing one set on each machine-weight station and then repeating the circuit one or two times. Circuit-training stations are frequently seen in parks and along jogging paths. There are stations for sit-ups, pull-ups, pushups, etc.

Elastic Bands: Surgical tubing or thick rubber bands that provide a strength-training workout by resisting when you try to stretch them.

Elliptical: These are also called cross-trainers and are machines that enable you to run or cross-country-ski in place. They provide low-impact exercise that is much easier on the feet and leg joints. The ski-type machines work the arms as well, so they provide an overall aerobic workout with components of strength training.

Fartlek: Most frequently used in running or walking, but can be applied to many activities. The purpose is to vary speed, distance and time randomly during a workout. For example, I start out jogging slowly for a couple minutes, then accelerate so that I'm at full speed at the end of the block, then walk for 50 yards, then jog slowly 100 yards, then sprint to the next fence post, etc. This is similar to "cross country" programs offered on some gym cardio machines.

Free Weights: These include dumb bells, bar bells, and weight plates stacked onto bar bells. Technically, kettle bells and medicine balls are free weights, too.

Interval Training: Varying of speed over set distances (or time). For example, jog one lap, walk one lap, repeat, in a consistent fashion. Interval training is almost always one of the program options on gym cardio machines.

Kettle Bell: Metal weights with a handle, varying in size and heaviness. They are used primarily in swinging motions.

Machine Weights: An apparatus with stacks of weights attached to cable and pulley systems.

Medicine Ball: A soft leather or rubber-covered ball manufactured in varying sizes and weights.

Pilates: Exercises designed to strengthen muscles, and improve balance, coordination and endurance. Pilates classes are held in most gyms and are available on inexpensive single DVDs or as part of a package of products.

Repetitions: ("Reps") A term used most often in strength training. It means the number of times you lifted a weight without stopping. "How many biceps curls did you do?" "I did 10 reps!"

Sets: Groups of repetitions, with rest or a different activity between each group to allow the muscle group being worked to recover briefly. "What are you doing on bench press today?" "I'm doing three sets of 10 with 2 minutes' rest."

Supersets: A series of sets in which each set exercises an opposing muscle group. For instance, I might superset chest and back exercises by doing one set of bench press followed immediately by one set of seated rows. Or I might superset sit-ups or any abdominal work with leg, back, chest or arm work. Supersets allow the worked muscle group to get rest; but the body stays active and the heart rate remains elevated.

Stability Ball: Big, bouncy, burst-proof balls that are used in core exercises. They come in several sizes and are often sold with complementary exercise DVDs and lightweight dumbbell sets.

Stair Climber: These are prevalent in most gymnasiums and come in two types: one works like an escalator, the other has steps that function independently. The independent step machines are easier on the knees and I find them to be more challenging. However, the escalator type is a good choice if you want to take stairs two-at-a-time or (for advanced users) walk backward or sideways.

Step Exercise: Frequently taught in a class but is also an "at-home" option. This is aerobic activity using platforms from several inches to a foot high. The platforms are stackable so one can adjust the step height to individual needs.

Cardio Equipment Training: The following designations are seen frequently on cardio activity machines in gyms. These simply refer to heart-rate levels and the amount of work related to them.

Fat-burning: Maintaining a heart rate of approximately 50 to 70 percent of maximum. This ensures the body burns primarily fatty acids for fuel, rather than glycogen. The lower your heart rate, the longer you should be able to continue your exercise without having to slow down or stop. Exercisers concerned primarily with weight loss and/or beginners work in this range.

Cardio: 70 to 85 percent of heart-rate maximum. At this level, the body burns both fatty acids and glycogen. Fatigue levels increase as work demands rise. Exercisers seeking to improve their endurance and heart strength work in this range.

Performance: 90 percent + of heart-rate maximum. I'm not recommending this for any reader. Performance level is only appropriate for serious athletes participating in highly competitive or professional sports.

Walking (brisk): I define this as walking as if you are late to an appointment.

Yoga: This is an activity that has spiritual, relaxation and meditational components. It focuses on balance, flexibility and strength in holding various positions. It's tougher than it looks, assuming you've never tried it. It is an excellent addition to the programs already outlined in this chapter. However, it is not recommended as your sole source of exercise.

APPENDIX B

Sample Exercise Programs[32]

Beginner: No Gym Required
Exercise: M, W, F or every other day. Maximum 5 days per week

Type	Description	Sets	Reps	Duration
Warm up	Walk slowly or march in place	1	varies	5 minutes
Warm up	Dynamic stretches	1	varies	20-30 seconds each
Warm up	Static stretches	1	varies	20-30 seconds each
Aerobic	Choose one or combine:	1	1	8-12 minutes min
	Brisk walk			20-30 minutes max
	Slow job			
	Gentle hill or stair climb			
	Swimming, yoga, Pilates (easy)			

---

32 Substitute or integrate calisthenics into the no-gym programs for a combination aerobic-strength workout. This is especially helpful if you're in a restricted space. Repeat as necessary.

Type	Description	Sets	Reps	Comment

Strength[33] *Not all exercises may be appropriate for you.*

Type	Description	Sets	Reps	Comment
Core	Sit-ups	1-2	10	
Core	Twists	1-2	20	At waist
Core	Side-bridge	1-2	5-10	"Push-up" from your side
Core	Crunches	1-2	10	

Chest/Back/Arms

	Description	Sets	Reps	Comment
	Push-ups	1-2	10	Bent-knee or plank
	Pull-ups	any	any	Part-way is OK
	Plank Pose	2	1	10-30 seconds
	Bench dips	1	3-5	As far as you feel comfortable

Legs/Butt/Calves/Feet

	Description	Sets	Reps	Comment
	Body weight squats	2	5-10	Use support as necessary
	Lunges	2	5-10	Each leg, as you're able
	Heel (or toe) raises	2	10	Use curb or block

Cool Down

	Description	Sets	Reps	Comment
	Walking and static stretches			5-10 minutes

---

33 Mix up the order in which you do the exercises listed here. They are grouped by type for informational purposes.

Beginner: Gym Access

Exercise: M, W, F or every other day. Maximum 5 days per week

Type	Description	Sets	Reps	Duration
Warm up	Walk treadmill, cycle, Elliptical	1	varies	5 minutes
Warm up	Dynamic stretches	1	varies	20-30 seconds each
Warm up	Static stretches	1	varies	20-30 seconds each
Aerobic	Choose one or combine: Treadmill, cycle, elliptical rowing machine, stair climber	1	1	8-12 minutes min 20-30 minutes max

Strength[34] *Not all exercises may be appropriate for you. Choose some from each category. Substitute and integrate.*

Core	Sit-ups	1-2	10	
Core	Twists	1-2	20	At waist
Core	Side-bridge	1-2	5-10	"Push-up" from your side
Core	Crunches	1-2	10	

Chest/Back/Shoulders/Arms

	Push-ups	1-2	10	Bent-knee or plank
	Pull-ups	any	any	Part-way is OK

---

34 Mix up the order in which you do the exercises listed here. They are grouped by type for informational purposes.

Type	Description	Sets	Reps	Comment
	Plank Pose	2	1	10-30 seconds
	Bench dips	1	3-5	As far as you feel comfortable
Chest	Bench press	2	10	
	Incline press	2	10	
Back	Lat pulls	2	10	
	Seated row	2	10	
Shoulders	Shoulder press	2	10	
Arms	Biceps curl	2	10	
	Triceps press	2	10	
Legs/Butt/Calves/Feet				
	Body weight squats	2	5-10	Use support as necessary
	Lunges	2	5-10	Each leg, as you're able
	Heel (or toe) raises	2	10	Toes or heel on curb
Legs	Leg press	2	10	
	Leg curl	2	10	
	Leg extension	2	10	
Calves	Seated/standing heel raise	2	10	

Cool Down

| | Walking and static stretches | | | 5-10 minutes |

Intermediate: No Gym Required
Exercise: M, T, W, Th, F or every other day. Maximum 5 days per week

Type	Description	Sets	Reps	Duration
Warm up	Walk slowly or march in place	1	varies	5 minutes
Warm up	Dynamic stretches	1	varies	20-30 seconds each
Warm up	Static stretches	1	varies	20-30 seconds each
Aerobic	Choose one or combine: Brisk walk Jog, swimming, hill or stadium stairs, dance, Pilates, exercise DVD. Fartlek/interval training	1	1	15-20 minutes min 30-35 minutes max

Strength[35] *Not all exercises may be appropriate for you.*

Core	Sit-ups	3	12-15	
Core	Twists	3	25	At waist
Core	Side-bridge	3	10-12	"Push-up" from your side
Core	Crunches	3	15	

---

35 Mix up the order in which you do the exercises listed here. They are grouped by type for informational purposes.

Type	Description	Sets	Reps	Comment
Chest/Back/Arms				
	Push-ups	3	12	Bent-knee or plank
	Decline push-ups	3	12	Feet on bench
	Pull-ups	any	any	Part-way is OK
	Plank Pose	2	1	45-60 seconds
	Bench dips	3	8-10	As far as you feel comfortable
Legs/Butt/Calves/Feet				
	Body weight squats	3	10-12	Use support as necessary
	Lunges	3	12-15	Each leg, as you're able
	Heel (or toe) raises	2	10	Use curb or block
Cool Down				
	Walking, slow jog and static stretches			5-10 minutes

Intermediate: Gym Access
Exercise: M, T, W, Th, F or every other day. Maximum 5 days per week

Type	Description	Sets	Reps	Duration
Warm up	Walk treadmill, cycle, elliptical	1	varies	5 minutes
Warm up	Dynamic stretches	1	varies	20-30 seconds each
Warm up	Static stretches	1	varies	20-30 seconds each
Aerobic	Choose one or combine: Treadmill, cycle, elliptical rowing machine, stair climber	1	1	15-20 minutes min 30-35 minutes max

Strength[36] *Not all exercises may be appropriate for you. Choose some from each category. Substitute and integrate.*

Core	Sit-ups	3	12-15	
Core	Twists	3	25	At waist
Core	Side-bridge	3	10-12	"Push-up" from your side
Core	Crunches	3	3	
Core	Roman chair	1-2	15	

---

36 Mix up the order in which you do the exercises listed here. They are grouped by type for informational purposes.

Type	Description	Sets	Reps	Comment
Chest/Back/Shoulders/Arms				
	Push-ups	3	12	Bent-knee or plank
	Pull-ups	any	any	Part-way is OK
	Plank Pose	2	1	45-60 seconds
	Bench dips	3	8-10	As far as you feel comfortable
Chest	Bench press	3	12	
	Incline press	3	12	
Back	Lat pulls	3	12	
	Seated row	3	12	
Shoulders	Shoulder press	3	12	
	Shrugs	3	12	
Arms	Biceps curl	3	12	
	Triceps press	3	12	
Legs/Butt/Calves/Feet				
	Body weight squats	2	10-12	Use support as necessary
	Lunges	3	12-15	Each leg, as you're able
Heel (or toe) raises		3	15	Toes or heel on curb
Legs	Leg press or squats	3	12	
	Leg curl	3	12	
	Leg extension	3	12	
	Dead-lift	3	10	
Calves Seated/standing heel raise		3	15	
Cool Down				
	Walking, slow jog, and static stretches			5-10 minutes

Advanced: No Gym Required
Exercise: M, T, W, Th, F or every other day. Maximum 5 days per week

Type	Description	Sets	Reps	Duration
Warm up	Slow jog inc light calisthenics	1	varies	5-7 minutes
Warm up	Dynamic stretches	1	varies	20-30 seconds each
Warm up	Static stretches	1	varies	20-30 seconds each
Aerobic	Choose one or combine: Brisk walk Jog, swimming, hill or stadium stairs, dance, Pilates, exercise DVD. Fartlek/interval training	1	1	20-25 minutes min 40-45 minutes max

Strength[37] *Not all exercises may be appropriate for you.*

Type	Description	Sets	Reps	Duration
Core	Sit-ups	3	15-20	
Core	Twists	4	25	From waist
Core	Side-bridge	3	10-12	"Push-up" from your side
Core	Crunches	3	15	

---

37 Mix up the order in which you do the exercises listed here. They are grouped by type for informational purposes.

Type	Description	Sets	Reps	Comment
Chest/Back/Arms				
	Push-ups	3	15-20	Bent-knee or plank
	Decline push-ups	3	15-20	Feet on bench
	Pull-ups	3	12	Part-way is OK
	Plank Pose	4	1	90 seconds
	Bench dips	3	15-20	As far as you feel comfortable
Legs/Butt/Calves/Feet				
	Body weight squats	4	15-20	Use support as necessary
	Lunges	3	15-20	Each leg, as you're able
	Heel (or toe) raises	3	20	Use curb or block
Cool Down				
	Walking, slow jog and static stretches			5-10 minutes

Advanced: Gym Access

Exercise: M, T, W, Th, F or every other day. Maximum 5 days per week

Type	Description	Sets	Reps	Duration
Warm up	Slow jog treadmill, cycle, elliptical, light calisthenics	1	varies	5-7 minutes
Warm up	Dynamic stretches	1	varies	20-30 seconds each
Warm up	Static stretches	1	varies	20-30 seconds each
Aerobic	Choose one or combine: Treadmill, cycle, elliptical, rowing machine, stair climber	1	1	20-25 minutes min 40-45 minutes max

Strength[38] *Not all exercises may be appropriate for you. Choose some from each category. Substitute and integrate.*

Core	Sit-ups	3	15-20	
Core	Twists	3	25	At waist
Core	Side-bridge	3	15	"Push-up" from side
Core	Crunches	3	3	
Core	Roman chair	1-2	15	

Chest/Back/Shoulders/Arms

	Push-ups	3	15-20	Bent-knee or plank
	Pull-ups	any	any	Part-way is OK
	Plank Pose	3	1	90 seconds
	Bench dips	3	15	As far as you feel comfortable

---

38 Mix up the order in which you do the exercises listed here. They are grouped by type for informational purposes.

Type	Description	Sets	Reps	Comment[39]
Chest	Bench press	3	15	
	Incline press	3	15	
Back	Lat pulls	3	15	
	Seated row	3	15	
Shoulders	Shoulder press	3	15	
	Shrugs	3	15	
Arms	Biceps curl	3	15	
	Triceps press	3	15	
Legs/Butt/Calves/Feet				
	Body weight squats	3	15-20	Use support as necessary
	Lunges	3	15	Each leg, as you're able
Heel (or toe) raises		3	20	Toes or heel on curb
Legs	Leg press or squats	3	15	
	Leg curl	3	15	
	Leg extension	3	15	
	Dead-lift	3	15	
Calves	Seated/standing heel raise	3	20	

Cool Down

Walking, slow jog, and static stretches   5-10 minutes

---

39   To build muscle and strength, use heavier weights, do more sets and fewer reps. Example 4 sets of 4-6 reps replaces 3 sets of 12-15 reps.

APPENDIX C

Dietary Information

Sample Menu approximating 2000 calories per day in 3-2-1 ratio

Meal	Food	Carb	Protein	Fat	Total[40]
Snack (270)	1-energy bar	154	80	36	270
Breakfast (390)	1-banana	87	3	<1	90
	2-boiled eggs	9	56	95	160
	2-multigrain rice cakes	115	12	11	140
Lunch (495)	4-oz. turkey breast	11	79	22	112
	2-slices raw tomato	7	<1	<1	7
	2-leafs romaine lettuce	7	3	<1	10
	2-slices multigrain bread	142	44	31	217

40   Source: United States Department of Agriculture's Research Service. Website research tool: http://ndb.nal.usda.gov/ndb/search/list

Meal	Food	Carb	Protein	Fat	Total
	1-tbsp light mayonnaise	4	<1	46	50
	1-Greek low fat yogurt	53	31	15	99
Snack (227)	1-apple	114	<1	<1	114
	1-oz. cheddar cheese slice	2	29	82	113
Dinner (593)	6-oz. skinless chicken breast	0	243	53	296
	2-cups asparagus	43	34	2	79
	1-cup brown rice	186	18	14	218
Snack (105)	1-cup 1% milk	53	33	18	105
TOTALS		987	665	425	2077
RATIOS		48%	32%	20%	

Examples are estimates, are for illustrative purposes and are dependent upon serving size, manufacturer and other factors.

Sample Menu approximating 1500 calories per day in 3-2-1 ratio

Meal	Food	Carb	Protein	Fat	Total[41]
Snack	1-Greek low fat yogurt	53	31	15	99
Breakfast (329)	2-oz shredded wheat	161	25	9	195
	½- cup 1% milk	27	17	9	53
	1-navel orange	77	4	<1	81
Lunch (290)	4-oz 1% low-fat cottage cheese	17	56	9	82
	2-cups seedless grapes	200	8	<	208
Snack	1-oz. almonds	12	12	58	82
Dinner (442)	6-oz fish (snapper)	<1	152	18	170
	1-cup mixed vegetable medley	98	20	<1	118
	6-oz baked red potato	138	16	<1	154
Snack	2-oz reduced fat peanut butter	48	40	99	187
	1-cup celery	16	<1	<1	16
TOTALS		847	381	217	1445
RATIOS		59%	26%	15%	

41 Source: United States Department of Agriculture's Research Service. Website research tool: http://ndb.nal.usda.gov/ndb/search/list

Sticking with It

As you can see from the examples, you don't need to be precise on the ratio or the calorie count. And most men will likely need more calories than 2000. So will some women. Dieters may like a 1500 calorie diet for several weeks to kick-start a weight loss program.

Use the tables as a guideline for taking charge of your diet and nutrition content. Create a diet that is based upon your base metabolic rate and an estimate of how many calories a day you burn. These burned-calories result from exercise, work (maybe you walk a lot on the job or work in construction) or other outdoor activities. Determine your goals. Are you trying to lose a couple pounds? Maintain current weight? Gain?

Do *not* make this an obsession. Estimating the numbers is fine. Or, if you're interested in keeping closer track, there are apps for that! Lots, in fact. For free.

Taking charge of your diet reinforces positive attributes such as planning and being proactive. It's your responsibility to find what works for you. Choose foods you like. Prepare or purchase items that work best in your budget and time schedule. And don't be afraid – in fact, I encourage this – to treat yourself to the occasional piece of cake or bowl of ice cream. This program of exercise and nutrition is worthless if you don't stick to it. And giving yourself those occasional rewards make you more likely to stick with it!

Time-Saver Tip

Build "cooking time" into your schedule two or three days a week. Pre-cook meats, rice or pasta. Clean and dice vegetables and fruits. Place them in plastic containers or freezer bags for later use. Have plenty of fresh (raw) fruit, carrots, celery, green beans, snap peas and broccoli cleaned and ready as snacks to satisfy cravings.

If you're not a cook, or you don't feel like you have time in your schedule to cook, there are many pre-packaged options that are healthy and microwavable and require an absolute minimum of prep work. READ THE FOOD LABELS! Watch for high levels of sodium and cholesterol.

APPENDIX D

Nutrition Reference

Essential Amino Acids

Arginine[42]

Involved in: Releasing growth hormone, regulating insulin, supporting our immune system, improving blood flow and promoting growth of sperm cells in men.

Supports: Wound healing and kidney function.

Found in: Peanuts, almonds walnuts, seeds (sunflower and flax), beans, tuna, chicken, salmon and shrimp.

Histidine

Involved in: Producing histamines which help us respond to attacks on our immune system. Histamines are used for treating allergic diseases, arthritis and anemia as low histamine levels are thought to play a role in these conditions.

---

42   This is a precursor to the neurotransmitter GABA. (1) Recall GABA is particularly affected by the use of alcohol and benzodiazepines.

Supports: Blood cell and tissue growth, including the insulating tissue (myelin) that surrounds nerve cell connections.

Found in: Soy protein, chicken; Swiss, parmesan, and Romano cheese, and provolone, egg and pork.

Isoleucine

Involved in: Producing hemoglobin, which carries oxygen and iron in our blood.

Supports: Strength, stamina and muscle strength.

Found in: Soy protein, eggs, milk, turkey, chicken, parmesan cheese, sesame and sunflower seeds, and fish.

Leucine

Involved in: Promoting the release of enkephelin, one of our natural opioids (pain killers) (1).

Supports: Healing, maintaining proper blood-sugar levels, slowing muscle breakdown and stimulating human-growth hormone.

Found in: Salmon, beef, chicken, soy beans, lentils, asparagus, eggs, walnuts, and flax seed.

Lysine

Involved in: Creating collagen, which supports healthy skin, hair, nails, teeth, tendons and muscles.

Supports: The body's ability to absorb calcium, burn fatty acids for energy and lower bad cholesterol.

Found in: Chicken, turkey, beef, fish, cream cheese, cottage cheese, soy and lentils.

Methionine

Involved in: Promoting the creation of creatine, the substance muscles use for energy.

Supports: Healthy skin, hair, nails; cardiovascular function; liver function. There is some evidence that it (taken as supplement L-Methionine) may help alleviate depression and arthritis.

Found in: Poultry, fish (including shellfish), beef, cream cheese, cottage cheese, cheddar cheese, eggs, beans, zucchini, turnip greens, soy, spinach, asparagus, sunflower and sesame seeds.

Phenylalanine

Involved in: Is converted to tyrosine, another amino acid. Tyrosine helps produce various brain chemicals, including epinephrine and norepinephrine (2), which affect energy and mood, respectively.

Supports: Phenylalanine deficiency looks a lot like PAW, with symptoms that include lack of energy, problems with memory and focus, thinking ability, depression and lack of appetite (2).

Found in: Beef, poultry, lamb, fish, soy, dairy, seeds (sunflower, sesame, and flax), walnuts, cashews, and peanuts.

Tryptophan[43]

Involved in: Is a precursor to serotonin, which we know as a neurotransmitter heavily impacted by our addictions. Serotonin deficiency is implicated in depression.

Supports: Relaxation, mood improvement and sleep.

Found in: Poultry, seafood, beef, dairy, eggs, cheese, and pumpkin seeds.

Valine

Involved in: Proper mental functioning and small intestine functioning, specifically in the assimilation of nutrients.

Supports: Muscle energy and helps to prevent muscle degradation by providing glucose during intense physical activity. Valine is also thought, along with methionine and threonine, to help reverse liver damage.

Found in: Dairy, eggs and soy.

Threonine

Involved in: Immune system function, muscle and connective tissue growth, and the ability of the liver to break down fatty acids.

Supports: Proper functioning of the central nervous system, healthy liver, muscle contraction. May support treating depression,

---

43 Many of you may know this as the chemical associated with becoming sleepy after Thanksgiving or other turkey-heavy meals.

multiple sclerosis (MS), and amyotrophic lateral sclerosis (ALS or Lou Gehrig's disease).

Found in: Meat, dairy, leafy green vegetables and grains.

Vitamins

Vitamin A

Important to: Healthy eyes and vision, especially night vision. Considered an anti-oxidant. Helps maintain healthy teeth, hair, skin and bones. Anti-oxidants are substances that thought to inhibit aging and promote disease prevention.

Deficiency produces: Poor vision, inflammation and/or dry eyes. Dry and rough skin. Susceptibility to infection.

Found in: Spinach, broccoli and other leafy greens; orange-colored foods, such as carrots, cantaloupe, pumpkins, and sweet potatoes[44]; and tomatoes, watermelon, cheddar and cream cheese, pecans and pistachios.

Vitamin A is fat-soluble.

Vitamin B or B Vitamin Complex[45]

B1 (thiamine) and B12 (cobalamin)

Important to: Nerve functioning.

---

44 Orange foods may or may not contain Vitamin A. But they all have beta-carotene (the source of the orange color) which our bodies convert into Vitamin A.

45   The B vitamins are numerous. All of the B-vitamins play a role in our ability to synthesize (metabolize) foods we eat and generate the energy we need to function. No doubt, you have seen many of these vitamins listed as additives to packaged foods you purchase.

Deficiency produces: Thinking and memory problems, muscle cramps and weakness (think about PAWs) and heart muscle problems.

B2 (riboflavin)

Important to: Healthy digestive processes, vision and hair growth; immune system function and the body's ability to heal.

Deficiency produces: Skin lesions, adrenal gland dysfunction, premature wrinkles; inflammation, swelling and cracking in the mouth and lips; burning and/or itching eyes; sensitivity to light.

B3 (niacin)

Important to: A healthy immune system and cholesterol levels.

Deficiency produces: Cognitive problems that look just like those in PAWs –Poor short-term memory, difficulty concentrating, problems with problem solving and abstract thinking.

B5 (pantothenic acid)

Important to: Healthy adrenal function. Also supports red blood cell growth.

Deficiency produces: Reduced output of epinephrine and norepinephrine which are critical to healthy energy levels and mood stabilization[46].

---

46 Another example of how deficiencies in vitamins and nutrients mimic and/or exaggerate PAW symptoms.

B6 (pyridoxine)

Important to: Proper functioning of the nervous and immune systems. Also promotes red blood cell and hemoglobin growth.

Deficiency produces: PAWs-like cognitive problems and disruption of thought-processes, anemia and depression.

B7 (biotin)

Important to: Nails, hair, and skin growth and vibrancy.

Deficiency produces: Dry or scaly skin or patchy dry skin. Dull hair. Fragile nails. Nervous system inefficiencies.

B9 (folic acid)

Important to: Proper physical growth, growth of red blood cells and hemoglobin, necessary to proper DNA functioning in the cells.

Deficiency produces: Anemia, depression, and gastro-intestinal disorders.

Various B-vitamins found in: Meat, dairy, poultry, cereals, beans, nuts, leafy green vegetables (spinach, Swiss chard, collard greens, mustard greens, etc.), avocado, fruits(berries, grapefruit, watermelon, pomegranate, mango, etc.) and foods fortified with B vitamins.

B vitamins are water-soluble.

Vitamin C

Important to: Ability to absorb calcium and iron. Strong immune system.

Deficiency produces: Lessened immune system resiliency, calcium and iron deficiencies, weakness. Extreme deficiencies can result in disease including scurvy[47].

Found in: citrus fruits (oranges, grapefruit), strawberries, kiwi, broccoli, Brussels sprouts, spinach, collard and mustard greens, and tomatoes.

Vitamin C is water-soluble.

Vitamin D[48]

Important to: Absorption of calcium and magnesium.

Deficiency produces: Weak bones, bone and muscle pain, osteoporosis, depressed mood, SAD (seasonal affective disorder.)

Found in: Eggs, tuna, salmon, mushrooms. Many foods including milk are fortified with D.

---

47   As you might recall from our history books, travelers to the New World often suffered scurvy due to the ships running out of fresh fruits and other foods containing Vitamin C. Scurvy is virtually unknown in the United States today, but results in bleeding into the skin, weakened gums and loose teeth.

48   This is a vitamin we produce can produce from sunlight, as well as absorb through foods we eat. Because of the rampant push in recent years to "cover up" and wear sunscreen whenever outdoors, doctors have found increasing cases of Vitamin D deficiency among children and adults. We can get the Vitamin D we need from about 30 minutes per day in the sun, with exposure of face and hands / upper arms. I'm not talking massive sunbathing here. We can do things in moderation and safely!

Vitamin D is fat-soluble.

Vitamin E

Important to: Cardiovascular health, immune system, sex drive and cognitive function. Supports healthy skin and hair.

Deficiency produces: Muscle weakness, pain and neurological problems, thinking difficulties, fertility problems, age spots.

Found in: Eggs, sunflower seeds, avocado, peanut butter, berries, almonds and hazelnuts. Many foods are fortified with Vitamin E.

Vitamin E is fat-soluble.

Vitamin K

Important to: The blood's ability to clot and prevent bleeding.

Deficiency produces: Bruising, bleeding, excessive menstrual bleeding, osteopenia and osteoporosis.

Found in: Leafy greens (spinach, Swiss chard, romaine lettuce), eggs, meats and fish. Intestinal bacteria can also produce Vitamin K, assuming uncompromised the enzyme and bacteria balance in our intestines, which is unlikely in alcohol and drug abusers.

Vitamin K is fat-soluble.

Minerals

Calcium

Important to: Fundamental building block of strong bones and teeth. Supports proper nerve transmission and muscular action, and the blood's ability to clot.

Deficiency produces: Brittle bones (osteoporosis), soft /malleable bones (rickets), blood-clotting problems, and cardiovascular and cognitive dysfunction.

Found in: Dairy, soybeans, dark leafy greens, and many fortified cereals and juices.

Iron

Important to: Quality and volume of red blood cells and hemoglobin (the molecule that carries oxygen in the bloodstream).

Deficiency produces: Fatigue, irritability, headache, difficulty concentrating and dizziness. (Note PAWs similarities.)

Found in: Red meat, dark green leafy vegetables, raisins, turkey, liver and beans.

Magnesium

Important to: Proper nerve cell transmission, muscle function, energy creation, protein synthesis and the body's ability to use potassium and calcium.

Deficiency produces: Weakness, fatigue, loss of appetite, and vomiting. More severe deficiencies can result in muscle cramps, nerve transmission problems and arrhythmia, particularly because of magnesium's role in the body's use of potassium and calcium. (4)

Found in: Avocado, peanuts, bananas, broccoli, potatoes, beans, salmon, chicken, raisins and rice.

Potassium

Important to: The regulation of proper nerve impulses, especially those related to heart rhythm.

Deficiency or excess produces: Too much or too little potassium can cause arrhythmia and heart attack. Other problems include: muscle cramps, digestion difficulties, fatigue, irritability, cognitive difficulties and dry skin. (Note the PAW symptoms among this list.)

Found in: Bananas, melons, meat, poultry, fish, milk, and citrus fruit.

Sodium

Important to: Maintaining fluid balance in the cells and proper nerve and muscle function.

Deficiency or excess produces: Retaining excess water (edema), high blood pressure, heart disease or failure, and stroke.

Found in: Potato chips, fast food, French fries, salad dressing, lunch meat, cheese, many canned goods (especially vegetables) and many microwave "healthy" meals.

About The Author

Rochelle "Shelley" Poerio, M.A., is a licensed alcohol & drug (LADC) counselor and an International Sports Sciences Association (ISSA) certified fitness trainer (CFT). She has also been in successful recovery from drug and alcohol abuse since September 5, 2001. *Rebalancing the Addictive Mind* is her first book.

Shelley's past history of substance abuse demonstrates that addiction can gain a powerful grip on anyone, no matter how normal or even promising her life might seem. Raised in a typical middle-class family, Shelley was a top student who would eventually attend Stanford University, which she paid for through a combination of working year-round, student loans and family support. She made the Stanford women's track team as a walk-on and was team captain her sophomore year.

At the same time, however, she suffered from a preoccupation with drugs and alcohol that dated to her first experimentations in high school. This compulsion would continue through college, into her subsequent career as a financial professional and – despite repeated offers of help from family and friends and multiple attempts at abstinence – for more than two decades of her adult life.

Finally, her physical and mental health at their absolute nadir, she checked herself into Inova Fairfax (Virginia) Hospital's Comprehensive Addiction Treatment Services (CATS) program on September 5, 2001, at age 40. Through treatment, hard work, regular participation in a 12-step program, and the love and care of her sponsor and countless people in her sober network, Shelley is now one of the success stories of addiction recovery.

In her ongoing life as a recovering addict, Shelley has focused on finding ways to help herself and others live happier, healthier, more meaningful lives. She began by volunteering with Big Sisters and at a local animal shelter. Eventually, her background in sports and personal insights gained from her own addiction treatment motivated her to use her unique experience as a way to help troubled youth and those with addiction-related problems.

She enrolled in Liberty University's graduate program in professional counseling and received her master's degree in 2012. Her thesis-oriented work explored the scientific basis of how exercise and nutrition support addiction recovery.

Shelley also began working, first as an intern and eventually as a certified substance-abuse counselor, with Vanguard Services Unlimited (now Phoenix Houses of the Mid-Atlantic) in Arlington, Virginia in 2009. She started an informal, strictly voluntary exercise group for resident adult-male clients, the majority of whom had been referred from the criminal justice system. She later developed this into an evidence-based fitness program.

The positive outcomes that arose from the program – including improved behaviors in group settings, fewer physically or verbally aggressive incidents, and improved client self-reports on mood, self-esteem, concentration and sleep – resulted in its permanent inclusion in the agency's residential treatment approach.

Her experience as a businesswoman convinced Shelley that exercise and nutrition for recovering addicts was a significantly neglected market niche. She recently founded Living Free Health & Fitness (LFHF), a non-profit corporation which utilizes the concepts in this book to support those with addictions, co-occurring disorders, aging or chronic disease –related needs, and members of the general public who are simply seeking healthier living options.

In addition to her position as president of LFHF, Shelley has a private practice as an addictions counselor and fitness trainer. She lives in Las Vegas, Nevada and actively practices the principles of this book.

References

Chapters Two, Three and Four

(1). Gerri, C., Pascual, M. (2009). Mechanisms involved in the neurotoxic, cognitive and neurobehavioral effects of alcohol consumption during adolescence. Elsevier Alcohol 44, 15-26. doi: 10.1016/jalcohol.2009.10.003

(2). Realini, N., Rubino, D., Parolaro, D. (2009) Neurological alterations at adult age triggered by adolescent exposure to cannabinoids. Pharmacological Research 60, 132-138. doi:10.1016/j.phrs.2009.03.006

(3). Lara, M. E. (2013). Pumped: Building a better brain through exercise and movement [DVD]. Haddonfield, NJ

(4). Inaba, D. S., & Cohen, W. E. (2007). Uppers downers and all arounders: Physical and mental effects of psychoactive drugs (6th ed.). Medford, OR: CNS Productions, Inc.

(5). Dumas, T.C. (March 2010). The ever-changing brain. The Ever-Changing Brain seminar presented for six hours' continuing education coursework at the Alexandria, Virginia Holiday Inn March 25, 2010.

(6). About.com (2010). Cingulate gyrus. Retrieved from http://biology.about.com/library/organs/brain/blcingyrus.htm   March 28, 2010.

(7). Storie, M. (2005). Basics of addiction counseling: desk reference and study guide. Alexandria, VA: NAADAC.

(8). McGovern, M. K. (2005). The effects of exercise on the brain. Paper presented at the Paper presented at Bryn Mawr College. Retrieved from http://serendip.brynmawr.edu/bb/neuro/neuro05/web2/>

(9). Foley, T. E. (2004). The Neurobiology of Addiction. (Dissertation). University of Colorado. Retrieved July 16, 2012 from http://search.proquest.com.ezproxy.liberty.edu:2048/docview/304861290

(10). Ratey, J. J. (2008). SPARK: The revolutionary new science of exercise and the brain. Little Brown & Company New York, NY

(11). The Economist. (4/12/2012). Fun run; Exercise and addiction. Retrieved July 16, 2012, from http://go.galegroup.com.ezproxy.liberty.edu:2048/ps/i.do?id=GALE%7CA286098235&v=2.1&u=vic_liberty&it=r&p=AONE&sw=w

(12). Brown, R. A., Abrantes, J. P., Marcus, B. H., Jakicic, J., Strong, D. R., Oakley, J. R.,...Gordon, A. A. (2009). Aerobic exercise for alcohol recovery: Rational, program description, and preliminary findings. Behavior Modification, (Dec 16 2008), 220-250. Perkinson and Jongsma (2006) doi:10.1177/0145445508329112

(13). Scerbo, F., Faulkner, G., Taylor, A., & Thomas, S. (2010). Effects of exercise on cravings to smoke: the role of exercise intensity and cortisol. Journal of Sports Sciences, 28(1), 11-19. doi:10.1080/02640410903390089

(14). Whitten, L. (2010). Physical activity reduces return to cocaine seeking in animal tests. NIDA Notes, 24(2), 9-11. Retrieved from National Institute for Drug Abuse website: http://go.galegroup.com.ezproxy.liberty.edu:2048/ps/i.do?id=GALE|A293353419&v=2.1&u=vic_liberty&it=r&p=AONE&sw=w

(15). Hosseini, M., Alaei, J. A., Naderi, A., Sharifi, M. R., & Zahed, R. (2009). Treadmill exercise reduces self-administration of morphine in male rats. Pathiophysiology, 16, 3-7. doi:10.1016/j.pathophys.2008.11.001

(16). Buchowski, M. S., Meade, N. N., Charboneau, E., Park, S., Dietrich, M. S., Cowan, R. L., Martin, P. R. (2011). Aerobic exercise training reduces cannabis craving and use in non-treatment seeking cannabis dependent adults. PLoS one, 6(3), 1-6. doi:10.1371/journal.pone.0017465

(17). Williams, D. J., & Strean, W. B. (2004). Physical activity as a helpful adjunct to substance abuse treatment. Journal of Social work Practice in the Addictions, 4(3), 83-100. doi:10.1300/J160v04n03_06

(18). Conner, B. T., Anglin, M. D., Annon, J., & Longshore, D. (2009). Effect of religiosity and spirituality on drug treatment outcomes. Journal of Behavioral Health Services & Research, 36:2, 189-198. Retrieved from http://ac.els-cdn.com/

S0740547206002066/1-s2.0-S0740547206002066- main.pdf?_tid= 652306fbac948f6def7e4b1edcea559b&acdnat=1338654313 _d71afd69e93baec88f82c5bb047c9d54

(19). Read, J. P., & Brown, R. A. (2003). The role of physical exercise in alcoholism treatment and recovery. Professional Psychology: Research and Practice, 34(1), 49-56. doi:10.1037/0735-7028.34.1.49

(20). Alcoholics Anonymous (2014). The big book. Alcoholics Anonymous World Services, Inc.

Chapter Five

(1). Hatfield (2011) Fitness: The complete guide (Edition 8.6.6). International Sports Sciences Association, Carpenteria, CA 93013

(2). Lara, M. E. (2013). Pumped: Building a better brain through exercise and movement [DVD]. Institute for Brain Potential. Haddonfield, NJ

(3). Inaba, D. S., & Cohen, W. E. (2007). Uppers downers and all arounders: Physical and mental effects of psychoactive drugs (6th ed.). Medford, OR: CNS Productions, Inc.

(4). Mayo Clinic. (13). Strength training: Getting stronger, leaner, healthier. Retrieved from http://www.mayoclinic.com/ health/strength-training/HQ01710

(5). Deuster, P. A., Singh, A., & Pelletier, P. A. (2007). The U.S. Navy SEAL guide to fitness and nutrition. New York, NY: Skyhorse Publishing, Inc.

(6). Koob, G. F. (2014). How the brain forms new habits: Why willpower is not enough [DVD]. Los Banos, CA

Chapters Six and Seven

(1). Hatfield (2011) Fitness: The complete guide (Edition 8.6.6). International Sports Sciences Association, Carpenteria, CA 93013

(2). Lara, M. E. (2013). Pumped: Building a better brain through exercise and movement [DVD]. Institute for Brain Potential. Haddonfield, NJ

(3). Williams, D. J., & Strean, W. B. (2004). Physical activity as a helpful adjunct to substance abuse treatment. Journal of Social Work Practice in the Addictions, 4(3)(2004), 83-100. doi:10.1300/J160v04n03_06

(4). Koob, G. F. (2014). How the brain forms new habits: Why willpower is not enough [DVD]. Los Banos, CA

(5). Althaus, C. B. (2001). Diet and addiction. Food Service Director 14, 10(62), Retrieved from ProQuest, October 5, 2012

(6). Blumenthal, D. M., & Gold, M. S. (2010). Neurobiology of food addiction. Current Opinion in Clinical Nutrition and Metabolic Care, 13, 359-365. doi:10.1097/MCO.0b013e32833ad4d4

(7). Brown, R. A., Abrantes, J. P., Marcus, B. H., Jakicic, J., Strong, D. R., Oakley, J. R.,...Gordon, A. A. (2009). Aerobic exercise for alcohol recovery: Rational, program description, and preliminary findings. Behavior Modification, (Dec 16 2008), 220-250.

(8). De Lisle, M. (2008). Special ops fitness training: High intensity workouts of Navy EALS, Delta Force, Marine Force Recon and Army Rangers. Berkeley, CA: Ulysses Press.

(9). Drug Addiction Treatment. (19). Exercise leads to positive results in recovery. Retrieved April 1, 2011, from http://www.drugaddictiontreatment.com/drug-addiction-treatments/exercise-leads-to-positive-results-in-recovery/

(10). Duester, P. A., Singh, A., & Pelletier, P. A. (2007). The U.S. Navy Seal guide to fitness and nutrition. New York, NY: Skyhorse Publishing.

(11). Editors Of Muscle & Fitness Hers (2007). 101 workouts for women. Woodland Hills, CA: Weider Publications LLC.

(12). Gale Group. Body image work leads to addiction recovery (1993). The Addiction Letter, (April, 1993), 1. Retrieved from http://find.galegroup.com.ezproxy.liberty.edu:2048/gtx/infomark.do?&contentSet=IAC-Documents&type=retrieve&tabID=T004&prodId=ITOF&docId=A13745668&source=gale&srcprod=ITOF&userGroupName=vic_liberty&versi on=1.0

(13). Inaba, D. S., & Cohen, W. E. (2007). Uppers downers and all arounders: Physical and mental effects of psychoactive drugs (6th ed.). Medford, OR: CNS Productions, Inc.

(14). Mayo Clinic. (2013). Strength training: Getting stronger, leaner, healthier. Retrieved from http://www.mayoclinic.com/health/strength-training/HQ01710

(15). McGovern, M. K. (2005, Spring). The effects of exercise on the brain. Retrieved April 9, 2011, from http://serendip.bryn-mawr.edu/bb/neuro/neuro05/web2/mmcgovern.html

(16). Miller, W.R., & Rollnick, S. (2002). Motivational interviewing: Preparing people for change. The Guilford Press. New York, NY.

(17). Millet, A. (28). Effects of exercise on substance abuse. Retrieved April 1, 2011, from http://www.livestrong.com/article/254285-effects-of-exercise-on-substance-abuse/

(18). Perkinson, R. R., & Jongsma, Jr., A. E. (2006). The addiction treatment planner (3rd ed.). Hoboken, NJ: John Wiley & Sons.

(19). Warrington, M. (23). The physical benefits of regular exercise. Retrieved April 9, 2011, http://www.associatedcontent.com/article/7887382/the_physical_benefits_of_regular_exercise.html

(20). Zangench, M., Barmaki, R., Ala-Leppilampi, K., & Peric, T. (2007). The potential role of physical exercise in addiction treatment and recovery: the social costs of substance misuse. Int J Ment Health Addiction, (20 July 2007), 210-218. doi: 10.1007/s11469-007-9111-7

Chapters Eight and Nine

(1). Jensen, B. (2000). Dr. Jensen's guide to body chemistry and nutrition. Lincolnwood, IL: Keats Publishing / NTC / Contemporary Publishing Group, Inc.

(2).University Of Maryland Medical Center. (June 7, 2011). Supplement phenylalanine. Retrieved from http://umm.edu/health/medical/altmed/supplement/phenylalanine

(3). WebMD. (2013). Glutamine overview. Retrieved from http://www.webmd.com/vitamins-supplements/ingredientmono-878-GLUTAMINE.aspx?activeIngredientId=878&activeIngredientName=GLUTAMINE

(4). National Institutes Of Health. (2013). Dietary supplements fact sheets: Strengthening knowledge and understanding of dietary supplements. Retrieved from http://ods.od.nih.gov/factsheets/Magnesium-HealthProfessional/

(5). Meule, A. (2011). How prevalent is food addiction? Frontiers in Psychiatry, 2(61), 1-4. doi: 10.3389/fpsyt.2011.0006

(6). Blumenthal, D. M., & Gold, M. S. (2010). Neurobiology of food addiction. Current Opinion in Clinical Nutrition and Metabolic Care, 13, 359-365. doi:10.1097/MCO.0b013e32833ad4d4

(7). Disalvo, D. (2012). What caffeine really does to your brain. Retrieved from http://www.forbes.com/sites/daviddisalvo/2012/07/26/what-caffeine-really-does-to-your-brain/

(8). Alcoholics Anonymous (2014). The big book. Alcoholics Anonymous World Services, Inc.

(9). Althaus, C. B. (2001). Diet and addiction. Foodservice Director, 14(10), 1-3. Retrieved from http://www.liberty.edu:2048/

login?url=http://search.proquest.com/docview/236420215?accou
ntid=12085

(10). Anonymous (2001). Nutrition and addictions. Canadian
Journal of Dietetic Practice and Research, Summer 2001(61), S8.

(11). Ballentine, R. (2007). Diet and nutrition: A holistic approach. Honesdale, PA: Himalayan Institute Press.

(12). Cass, H. (2002). Overcoming addiction. Total Health,
24(5), 36-37. Fuchs, J. (1999). Alcoholism, malnutrition, vitamin
deficiencies and the skin. Clinics in Dermatology, 17, 457-461. doi:
PII S0738- 081X(99)00032-2

(13). Grotzkyj-Giorgi, M. (2009). Nutrition and addiction: Can
dietary changes assist with recovery? Drugs and Alcohol Today,
9(2), 24-28.

(14). Lakhan, S. E., & Vieira, K. F. (2010). Nutritional and herbal
supplements for anxiety and anxiety-related disorders: Systematic
review. Nutrition Journal, 9(42), 2-14. doi:10.1186/1475-2891-9-42

(15). Langer, S. (1998). Extinguishing addictions: Mind, body
and nutrition. Better Nutrition, 60(9), 48-52. Retrieved from
http://www.liberty.edu:2048/login?url=http://search.proquest.
com/docview/194173743?accountid=12085

Chapter Ten

(1). Alcoholics Anonymous (2014). The big book. Alcoholics
Anonymous World Services, Inc.

(2). Bing Search Engine Dictionary. (2014). Retrieved from http://www.bing.com/search?q=define+spirit&qs=n&form=QBLH&pq=define+spirit&sc=8-13&sp=-1&sk=&cvid=3dbb4d4e87cb4b588368ac13d509af94

(3). Dictionary.Com. (2014). Spiritual. Retrieved from http://dictionary.reference.com/browse/spiritual

(4) Entwistle, D. N. (2010). Integrative approaches to psychology and Christianity: An introduction to worldview issues, philosophical foundations, and models of integration (2nd ed.). Eugene, OR: Cascade Books.

(5) Hall, J. H., & Fincham, F. D. (2005). Self-forgiveness: the stepchild of forgiveness research. Journal of Social and Clinical Psychology, 24(5), 621-637.

(6) Hawkins, R., & Rice, D. (2012, February). Constructing a comprehensive theory of counseling. Paper presented at the Liberty University. Lynchburg, VA.

(7). Priester, P. E., Scherer, J., Steinfeldt, J. A., Jana-Masri, A., Jashinsky, T., Jones, J. E., Vang, C. (2009). The frequency of prayer, meditation and holistic interventions in addictions treatment: A national survey. Pastoral Psychology, 58, 315-322. doi:10.1007/s11089-009-0196-8

(8) Wikipedia. (2014). Spirit. Retrieved from http://en.wikipedia.org/wiki/Spirit

Essential Amino Acids

(1). Jensen, B. (2000). Dr. Jensen's guide to body chemistry and nutrition. Lincolnwood, IL: Keats Publishing / NTC / Contemporary Publishing Group, Inc.

(2). University Of Maryland Medical Center. (June 7, 2011). Supplement phenylalanine. Retrieved from http://umm.edu/health/medical/altmed/supplement/phenylalanine

Minerals

(4). National Institutes Of Health. (2013). Dietary supplements fact sheets: Strengthening knowledge and understanding of dietary supplements. Retrieved from http://ods.od.nih.gov/factsheets/Magnesium-HealthProfessional/

54635172R00127

Made in the USA
Lexington, KY
22 August 2016